The
Triumphant Cat

The Triumphant Cat; an Anthology of Verse, Prose, & Pictures; Gathered from the Ancient & Modern Authors; Selected, & Edited by Marmaduke Skidmore, Esquire

ROBINSON PUBLISHING   LONDON

Robinson Publishing Ltd.
7, Kensington Church Court
London w8 4sp

First published by Robinson Publishing Ltd. 1993

A copy of the British Library Cataloguing in Publication Data for this title is available from the British Library.

ISBN 1-85487-241-9

Design adapted to this format by Jonathan Newdick

Printed and bound by Arnoldo Mondadori Editore, Italy

To my dear
Friends
Celia and Jan

CONTENTS

XIII

APPENDIX.

PREFACE.

WHEN the great Dinosaurs disappeared mysteriously from the face of the Earth, the ancestor of the Modern Cat, or *Felis sapiens*, was a small, long-tailed, sharp-toothed and sharper-clawed, bewhiskered, tree-climbing, carnivorous mammal, the Miacid. This primitive, though intelligent, creature flourished some fifty million years ago; and from it descended the Sabre-Toothed Tiger, the Cave Lion, the Cat, the Walrus, and the Sealion. The Walrus and the Sealion abandoned the cat race and became drop-outs; but the more competitively-minded felines kept to land and ruled the Earth for forty million years, striking terror even into the Rhinoceros and the Elephant, fully justifying the proud title:

I

King of Beasts. This was the Golden Age.

Long was this glorious reign; but, as is the way of all reigns, at last, it met a challenger —Man.

Primitive Man, or *Homo silvestris*, though less powerful than the Sabre-Toothed Tiger and less intelligent than the Cat, possessed certain primitive skills, such as weapon-making, which threatened Cat-rule. The Sabre-Toothed Tiger and the Cave Lion responded to the threat by a war aimed at Man's total extermination. In this, however, they were less than wholly successful; for it was the Sabre-Toothed Tiger, rather than Man, that became extinct.

Felis sapiens, pondering this *débâcle*, perceived that the solution to the problem lay not in the destruction of Man as such, but in the destruction of Man *as the enemy*. The Cat, therefore, embarked on the heroic experiment of taming and civilizing Man, of converting *Homo silvestris* into *Homo domesticus*.

The experiment was triumphantly successful; and, by 3000 B.C., we find Egyptian Man tamed and civilized and the friend and servant of the Cat, who lives an honoured guest in his house; — indeed, so impressed was Egyptian Man by the superior intelligence and virtues of the Cat, that he — very naturally — worshipped the Cat as a God. In China, too, the Cat brought civilization; and at least as early as 1000 B.C. he was welcomed in the Chinese home, where he was supposed the God of Fertility, Li-shou.

Civilization and the Cat came somewhat later to Greece; and no mention of the Cat is made in either Homer or Plato. He appears, however, on late Greek vases and in the plays of Aristophanes; and legend associates him with Diana and the Moon. In Rome, the Cat was worshipped as the God of Liberty and is held in high esteem there to this day. With the Romans, the Cat appeared in Britain, having, as one Cat historian has put it, "marched with the Legions".

With the coming of the Barbarians and the Fall of Rome the Cat fled to the Imperial Courts of Byzantium and the monastic cities of Ireland, where the

lamps of learning and culture still flick-
ered; — as also among the sophas of Islam,
where, favoured by the Prophet, the Cat
prospered.

In Western Europe during the Middle
Ages, the Cat, though admired and loved
by the more cultivated, such as Petrarch
and Chaucer, aroused fear and hostility
among the ignorant and superstitious, who
persecuted him as an ally of Satan. In con-
sequence, the Rat and the Plague Flea
flourished; and, during the Black Death,
the population of Europe was reduced to
a half. Such are the results of persecut-
ing the Cat.

Come the Renaissance, when Curiosity
became the supreme virtue, the Cat returned to a popularity which reached its height
in the Eighteenth Century. Indeed, the Aug-
ustan Ideals of Reason, Politeness, Elegance,
and Toughness seem epitomized in the Cat.
Lord Chesterfield had no need to instruct
his polished cat in the Graces; nor Dr Johnson to teach Hodge commonsense. In France
too, no *salon* was complete without its
philosophe cat; and, as a favourite of
Louis XV's Queen, the Cat settled himself

firmly upon the scented silken cushions of Versailles.

With the French Revolution, the *aristo* Cat was forced to become an *émigré* Cat and join his British Cat cousin embattled against the notorious Cat-hater Bonaparte.

As we all know, the Cat finally defeated Boney; but Civilization and the Cat have never fully recovered from the revolutionary upheaval; and the struggle between Civilization and Barbarism continues. Queen Victoria, the Brontës, Wagner, President Lincoln, Edward VII, Bernard Shaw, H.G. Wells, Thomas Hardy, Dr Schweitzer, Einstein, and Winston Churchill are among the Cat-lovers: Kipling, Hitler, Stalin, Enoch Powell, and President Nixon are not.

However, should Barbarism win, should Man, with his now notorious talent for weapon-making, finally destroy himself in an Atomic Cataclysm, he will only have accomplished what the Sabre-Toothed Tiger attempted so many thousands of years ago. And the Cat, armed with forty million years' experience of running the world — not to mention his Nine Lives —, will no doubt survive and pick up the reins of world-government from where he let 'em drop.

For he is a very Cool Cat indeed.

In the following pages I present a selection of Eminent Cats and Cat-lovers — together with a handful of *Cat-haters* — for the instruction and amusement of my many human friends.

The illustrations are mostly taken from contemporary sources. I am indebted to my friend Walter Payne for many invaluable suggestions.

MARMADUKE SKIDMORE.

Chester, August, 1974.

WHO IS THIS CAT?

I AM the Cat which fought hard by the Acacia Tree in Heliopolis on the night when the foes of the Setting Sun were destroyed.

Who is this Cat?

This male Cat is the Sun-god Ra himself and he was called Mau because of the speech of the God Sa concerning him: He is like unto that which he hath made, therefore did the name Ra become Mau. Others, however, say that the male cat is Shu, the God of the Air, who made over the possessions of the Earth-god Geb to Osiris.

As concerning the fight which took place near the Acacia Tree in Heliopolis these words refer to the slaughter of the children of rebellion, when righteous retribution was meted out to them for

7

the evil they had done. As concerning the night of the battle these words refer to the invasion of the eastern portion of the heavens by the children of rebellion, whereupon a great battle arose in heaven and in all the earth.

From *The Book of the Dead*, before 3000 B.C.

THOU ART THE GREAT CAT

P RAISE be to thee, O Ra, exalted Lion-god, thou art the Great Cat, the Avenger of the Gods and the Judge of Words, the President of the Sovereign Chiefs and the Governor of the Holy Circle; thou art indeed the bodies of the Great Cat.

From *The Seventy-five Praises of Ra*, circa 1700 B.C.

THE BEAUTIFUL CAT

THE beautiful cat which endures, which endures.

From the Stela of Nebra, *circa* 1600 B.C.

BAST

BAST, the cat-headed goddess of Bubastis, rose from the lowly position of a purely local deity to be one of the most popular divinities of Egypt. The fact that she was in origin a local goddess shows that her cult was very early; a further proof is that her city took its name from her temple. Bubastis was an important centre among the principalities of the Delta in early historic times, so important that the great Khufu was responsible for some of the building of her temple.

Bast was known and worshipped in other parts of Egypt beside her own little kingdom, but the great wave of cat-worship did not occur till the XXII dynasty, when Shishak I, the then prince of Bubastis, suddenly rose to power and became the Pharaoh. Then his local deity rose with him, and her cult was popularised throughout the country, and she remained one of the most important deities when Greek travellers and authors began to frequent Egypt.

Dr Margaret A. Murray.

EGYPTIAN CATS.

THE number, already large, of domestic animals would have been greatly increased were it not for an odd thing that happens to the cats. The females, when they have kittens, avoid the toms, greatly to the distress of the latter who are thus deprived of their satisfaction. The toms, however, get over the difficulty very ingeniously, for they either openly seize, or secretly steal, the kittens and kill them—but without eating them—and the result is that the females, deprived of their kittens and wanting more (for their maternal instinct is very strong), go off to look for mates again. What happens when a house catches fire is most extraordinary: nobody takes the least trouble to put it out, for it is only the cats that matter; everyone stands in a row, a little distance from his neighbour, trying to protect the cats, who nevertheless slip through the line, or jump over it, and hurl themselves into the flames. This causes the Egyptians deep distress. All the inmates of a house where a cat has died a natural death shave their eyebrows....Cats which have died are taken to Bubastis, where they are embalmed and buried in sacred receptacles....

Herodotus, *circa* 484 — 424 B.C.

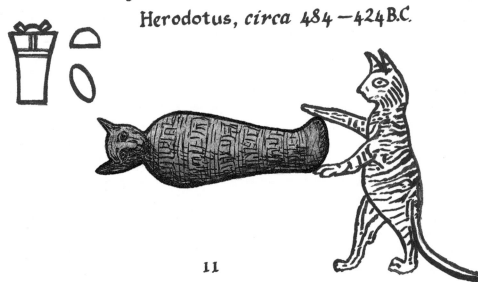

11

DEATH PENALTY FOR CAT-KILLING

AND because of their fear of such a punishment any who have caught sight of one of these animals lying dead withdraw to a great distance and shout with lamentations and protestations that they found the animal already dead. So deeply implanted also in the heart of the common people is their superstitious regard for these animals and so unalterable are the emotions cherished by every man regarding the honour due to them that once, at the time when Ptolemy their king had not as yet been given by the Romans the appelation of "friend" and the people were exercising all zeal in courting the favour of the embassy from Italy which was then visiting Egypt and, in their fear, were intent upon giving no cause for complaint or war, when one of the Romans killed a cat and the multitude rushed in a crowd to his house, neither the officials sent by the king to beg the man off nor the fear of Rome which all the people felt were enough to save the man from punishment, even though his act had been an accident. And this incident we relate, not from hearsay, but we saw it with our own eyes on the occasion of the visit we made to Egypt.

Diodorus, 50 B.C.

METAMORPHOSIS

A CAT was enamoured of a handsome youth and begged Aphrodite to change her into a woman. The goddess, pitying her sad state, transformed her into a beautiful girl, and when the young man saw her he fell in love with her and took her home to be his wife. While they were resting in their bedroom, Aphrodite, who was curious to know if the cat's instincts had changed along with her shape, let a mouse loose in front of her. She at once forgot where she was, leapt up from the bed, and ran after the mouse to eat it. The indignant goddess then restored her to her original shape.

Æsop, 500 B.C.?

THE LION'S AUNT

THE cat is older than the lion in the order of creation. It is told that the lion, new-created in all his strength and beauty, was yet lacking in skill and wisdom. Accordingly, he was sent for education to the cat. She taught him nearly everything she knew — to stalk, to wait, to pounce, to kill. One day, the lion thought to exercise these skills on his preceptress, so much smaller than himself. He prepared to spring and kill; but there was just one art that the cat had not taught him. She ran up a tree, and so saved herself by exercising that one art. To this day, the cat is known as the lion's aunt, even by people who do not know that she is so called because she was, though smaller and weaker, a little older and wiser than the lion.

Arab legend.

BUDDHA'S BLESSING

WHEN the Lord Buddha called all the animals to be blessed the cat did not bother to turn up, and so alone remained unblessed among the animals.

Indian legend.

THE FALSE YOGI

A RAT and a bird had pounced simultaneously on a titbit of food. Neither was strong enough to wrest the prize from the other, and neither could defeat the other in argument. Accordingly, they decided to take the case to arbitration. Near at hand sat a contemplative cat, still, quiet, thoughtful — apparently meditating on the eternal verities. They begged the cat for a righteous decision and the cat, sure enough, told them that such a decision must depend on a proper interpretation of the holy scripture. He embarked on a long exposition of texts and their theological and moral implications, so that at length both rat and bird, lacking a Scottish congregation's appetite for sermons, were nodding off to sleep. At this point, the cat, watchful behind his air of holy detachment from this world, pounced — and cleared the board.

Indian legend.

JULIUS CAESAR AND OTHERS

THE cat is probably capable of inspiring a greater degree of loathing than any other animal and when this sentiment becomes acute — often resulting in sweating, paleness, nausea, hysteria, and even fainting — it is called *ailurophobia*.

Julius Caesar was among the great men who abhorred cats. Two French Kings, Henry II and Charles IX, swooned if a cat came too close. Napoleon sweated profusely in the presence of cats, and Field-Marshal Lord Roberts, the hero of Afghanistan and the South African War, could not breathe properly in their company.

Ronsard, the gentle and civilized poet, said of himself:

There is no man now living anywhere
Who hates cats with a deeper hate than I;
I hate their eyes, their heads, the way they stare,
And when I see one come I turn and fly.

International Encyclopedia of Cats.

MAHOMET AND OTHERS

MAHOMET so loved his cat that once when it lay sleeping against his arm and he was called away, he cut off the sleeve of his robe rather than disturb it.

It is also related that Mahomet said, "Cats are not impure; they keep watch around us." He used water from which a cat had drunk for his purifications, and his wife, Ayishah, ate from a vessel from which a cat had eaten. And when Mahomet desired to honour his faithful follower Abd-er-rahim, he gave him the title of Abuhareira, which means "Father of the Cat".

Goethe refers to Mahomet's cat in Paradise:

Here purrs Abuhareira's cat
　　Round him, with coaxings bland;
A holy creature sure is that
　　Stroked by the Prophet's hand.

Christabel Aberconway, *A Dictionary of Cat Lovers*

THE EMPRESS WU CHAU, HER CAT, AND HER PARROT

DURING the time of the Empress Wu, a cat and a parrot were trained to eat food from the same vessel. The Empress ordered Censor P'eng Hsien-chueh to supervise the exhibition of their friendliness to all the officials at the Court and the Commissioners of the Empire. But before the exhibition was over, the cat became hungry and accordingly ate the parrot. The Empress Wu was very much embarrassed.

Chang Tsu, 660 – 741 A.D.

PANGUR BÁN

I AND Pangur Bán, my cat,
'Tis a like task we are at;
Hunting mice is his delight,
Hunting words I sit all night.

Better far than praise of men
'Tis to sit with book and pen;
Pangur bears me no ill-will,
He too plies his simple skill.

'Tis a merry thing to see
At our tasks how glad are we,
When at home we sit and find
Entertainment to our mind.

Oftentimes a mouse will stray
In the hero Pangur's way;
Oftentimes my keen thought set
Takes a meaning in its net.

19

'Gainst the wall he sets his eye
Full and fierce, and sharp and sly;
'Gainst the wall of knowledge I
All my little wisdom try.

When a mouse darts from its den,
O how glad is Pangur then!
O what gladness do I prove
When I solve the doubts I love!

So in peace our tasks we ply,
Pangur Bán, my cat, and I;
In our arts we find our bliss,
I have mine and he has his.

Practice every day has made
Pangur perfect in his trade;
I get wisdom day and night,
Turning darkness into light.

Anonymous VIII century Irish monk, translated
from the Irish by Dr Robin Flower.

HUNGRY MASTER AND HUNGRY CAT.

WHEN my house was bare of skins and pots of
    meal,
after it had been inhabited, not empty, full of folk
    and richly prosperous,
I see the mice avoid my house, retiring to the gov-
    ernor's palace.
The flies have called for a move, whether their
    wings are clipped or whole.
The cat stayed a year in the house and did not see
    a mouse,
shaking its head at hunger, at a life full of pain
    and spite.
When I saw the pained downcast head, the heat in
    the belly, I said,
"Patience; you are the best cat my eyes ever saw in
    a ward."
He said, "I have no patience. How can I stay in a
    desert like the belly of a she ass?"

I said, "Go in peace to a hotel where travellers are
    many and much trade,
Even if the spider spins in my wine jar, in the jug,
    and the pot.

Abu Shamaqmaq, *circa 770* A.D. translated from
the Arabic by Dr A. S. Tritton.

FREIA.

AMONG the gods of Norse mythology,
Freia, the Goddess of Love, Youth and
Eternal Rebirth, habitually rode a flying cat

22

through the air on her numerous journeys. She had an arrangement with Wotan to collect half the warriors slain in battle to entertain with feasting and beer, and hydromel and fun, in her palace of Volkvang;—the other half went with Wotan to Valhalla. She is sometimes, as the newspapers say, "described as" Wotan's wife; but it seems that though at one time she was Wotan's *very good friend and permanent house-guest*, she had too many other very good friends for his taste; —he could be a bit stuffy at times—and perhaps he got sick of all those cats crawling about the place. Be that as it may, she certainly appears in *Rheingold*—but *without her cats.*—What an opportunity Wagner—a keen animal-lover himself and the possesser of *two* cats (besides two peacocks, a parrot, and a horse)—missed in failing to add Freia's cat to his operatic zoo!

Freia, incidently, is famous for her Day, Freia's Day or Friday.

THE EMPRESS ZOË, 980—1054

ON succeeding her father, Constantine IX, the Empress Zoë, at the age of forty-eight, married a Patrician who thereupon

assumed the title of Romanus III. Him she
murdered in 1034 and married her favourite
Chamberlain (Michael IV), thus justifying the
Roman belief that every adulteress is capable
of poisoning her husband. At his death, seven
years later, he was succeeded by his nephew
Michael, who at once seized and imprisoned
the Empress. Within a year, however, this
upstart was dethroned, and the Empress, dau-
ghter of so many emperors, was reinstated.
A few months later, being then over sixty years
of age, the indefatigable Zoë married for the
third time. Her last husband, Constantine
X, outlived her.

Whatever her faults, it appears that the Empress Zoë treated her cat suitably. Having a
passion for making scents, her own room was
kept at an unbearable heat owing to the furn-
aces she used, so that her cat enjoyed excess-

ive warmth and sweet scents, which all cats love. It is also stated that her cat ate at the Imperial table from gold plate.

Christabel Aberconway, *A Dictionary of Cat Lovers*

"SECOND ONLY TO LAURA"

DURING the last years of his life, Petrarch (1304 –1374), the poet and pioneer of mountain climbing, lived in peaceful retire- ment in Arqua with, as his companion, a gift- ed cat, whom he praised as "second only to Laura."

SWICH APPETYT

LAT take a cat, and fostre him well with milk, And tendre flesh, and make his couche of silk, And lat him seen a mous go by the wall; Anon he weyveth milk, and flesh, and al, And every deyntee that is in that hous, Swich appetyt hath he to ete a mous.

Geoffrey Chaucer, 1340?–1400.

SIR HENRY WYATT'S CAT

AS a young man, Sir Henry Wyatt (1460–
1537), the father of the poet, was imprison
by Richard III for his loyalty to the Lancastrian
party:

Hee was imprisoned often, once in a cold and
narrow Tower, where hee had neither bed to
lie on, nor cloaths sufficient to warme him,
nor meate for his mouth; hee had starved
there, had not God sent a cat both to feede and
warm him:— itt was his own relation unto
them, from whom I had it; a cat came one day
into the Dungeon unto him; and as it were offered herself unto him, hee was glad of her,
laid her in his bosom to warm him, and by making much of her, won her love; after this, shee
would come every day unto him, divers times,
and when shee could gett one, bring him a
pigeon; hee complain'd to his keeper of his
cold, and short fare, the answer was hee durst
not better itt; but said Sir Henry, if I can
provide any, will you promise to dresse itt for
mee; I may well enough (said the keeper) you
are safe for that matter — and being urged
againe, promised him, and kept his promise
— dressed for him from time to time such pigeons as the cat provided for him. Sir Henry

Wyat in his prosperity would ever make much
of a cat....   Thomas Scott of Egreston Esq.

This Knight with hunger, cold, and care, neere
   starved, pincht, pyn'de away;
I sillie Beaste did feed, heate, cheere, with dyett,
   warmth, and playe.

                Sir Thomas Wyatt? 1503? —1542.

A CAT OF CARLYSHE KYNDE

THAT vengeaunce I aske and crye,
   By way of exclamacyon,
On all the hole nacyon
Of cattes wylde and tame;
God send them sorowe and shame!
That cat specyally
That slew so cruelly
My lytell prety sparowe
That I brought vp at Carowe.
   O cat of carlyshe kynde,
The fynde was in thy mynde
Whan thou my byrde vntwynde!

                John Skelton, 1460? —1529.

27

ADVICE ON CATS

THOUGH cat (a good mouser) is jewel in house,
Yet ever in dayry have trappe for a mouse.

Thomas Tusser, 1524?—1580.

PUSSY CAT, PUSSY CAT

PUSSY cat, pussy cat, where have you been?
I've been to London to look at the queen.
Pussy cat, pussy cat, what did you there?
I frightened a little mouse under her chair.

PUSSICAT, WUSSICAT

PUSSICAT, wussicat, with a white foot,
When is your wedding, and I'll come to it.
The beer's to brew, the bread's to bake,
Pussy cat, pussy cat, don't be late.

Traditional.

28

EPITAPH ON A PET CAT

MY life seems dull and flat,
And, as you'll wonder what,
Magny, has made this so,
I want you first to know
It's not for rings or purse
But something so much worse:
Three days ago I lost
All that I value most,
My treasure my delight;
I cannot speak or write,
Or even think of what
Belaud, my small grey cat,
Meant to me, tiny creature,
Masterpiece of nature
In the whole world of cats —
And certain death to rats! —
Whose beauty was worthy
Of immortality.

Belaud, first let me say,
Was not entirely grey
Like cats bred here at home,
But more like those in Rome,
His fur being silver-grey
And fine and smooth as satin,
While, lying back, he'd display
A white expanse of ermine

Small muzzle, tiny teeth;
Eyes of a tempered warmth,
Whose pupils of dark-green
Showed every colour seen
In the bow which splendidly
Arches the rainy sky.

Plump neck, short ears, height
To his head proportionate;
Beneath his ebony nostrils
His little leonine muzzle's
Prim beauty, which appeared
Fringed by the silvery beard
Which gave such waggish grace
To his young dandy's face.

His slender leg, small foot —
No lambswool scarf could be
More soft, except when he
Unsheathed and scratched with it!
His neat and downy throat,
Long monkey's tail, and coat
Diversely flecked and freckled,
In natural motley speckled;
His flank and round stomach
Under control, his back
Longish — a Syrian
If ever there was one!

30

This was Belaud, a gentle
Animal, whose title
To beauty was so sure
He'd no competitor!
A sad and bitter cross!
Irreparable loss!
It almost seems to me
That Death, though he must be
More ruthless than a bear,
Would, if he'd known my rare
Belaud, have felt his heart
Soften — and for my part
I would not wince and shrink
So from life's joys, I think.

But Death has never watched
Him as he jumped or scratched,
Laughed at his nimble tricks,
His many wild frolics,
Admired the sprightly grace
With which he'd turn, or race,
Or, with one whirl of cat,
Tumble, or seize a rat
And play with it — and then
Would make me laugh again
By rubbing at his jaw
With such a frisky paw
In such a dashing manner!

Or when the little monster
Leapt quietly on my bed,
Or when he took his bread
Or meat most daintily
Straight from my lips — for he
Showed in such various ways
His quaint, engaging traits!

What fun to watch him dance,
Scamper, and skate, and prance
After a ball of thread;
To see his silly head
Whirl like a spinning wheel
After his velvet tail;
Or, when he made of it
A girdle, and would sit
Solemnly on the ground,
Showing his fluffy round
Of paunch, seeming to be
Learned in theology,
The spit of some well-known
Doctor at the Sorbonne!
And how, when he was teased,
He used to fence with us —
Yet if we stopped to fuss
Was very soon appeased!

O Magny, now you see

How he diverted me,
You'll realize why I mourn —
And surely no cat born
Has ever had so nice
A style with rats and mice!

He would come unawares
Upon them in their lairs,
And not one could escape
Unless he'd thought to scrape
A second hole — no rat
Ever outran that cat!
And let me add at once
My Belaud was no dunce,
But very teachable,
Knowing how to eat at table —
When offered food, that is:
That eager paw you'd see,
Held out so flirtingly,
Might scratch you otherwise!

Belaud was well-behaved
And in no way depraved;
His only ravages
Were on an ancient cheese,
A finch, and a young linnet
Whose trillings seemed to get
On Belaud's nerves — but then

How perfect are we men?

He wasn't the sort to be
Out everlastingly
After more food to eat,
But was content to wait
Until his meals, when he
Ate without gluttony.

Also he was by nature
A well conducted creature;
For he would never spread
His traces far and wide
Like many cats, but tried
To live as a well-bred
Feline should live and be
In all his ways cleanly...

He was my favourite plaything;
And not for ever purring
A long and tunelessly
Grumbling litany,
But kept in his complainings
To kitten-like miaowings.

My only memory
Of him annoying me
Is that, sometimes at night

When rats began to gnaw
And rustle in my straw
Mattress, he'd waken me
Seizing most dexterously
Upon them in their flight.

Now that the cruel right hand
Of Death comes to demand
My bodyguard from me,
My sweet security
Gives way to hideous fears;
Rats come and gnaw my ears,
And mice and rats at night
Chew up the lines I write!

The gods have sympathy
For poor humanity;
An animal's death foretells
Some evil that befalls,
For heaven can speak by these
And other presages.
The day fate cruelly
Took my small dog from me —
My Peloton — the sense
Of evil influence
Filled me with utter dread;
And then I lost my cat:
What crueller storm than that

Could break upon my head!

He was my very dear
Companion everywhere
My room, my bed, my table,
Even more companionable
Than a little dog; for he
Was never one of those
Monsters that hideously
Fill the night with their miaows;
And now he can't become,
Poor little puss, a tom —
Sad loss, by which his splendid
Line is abruptly ended.

God grant to me, Belaud,
Command of speech to show
Your gentle nature forth
In words of fitting worth,
Your qualities to state
In verse as delicate,
That you may live while cats
Wage mortal war on rats.

Joachim du Bellay, 1525 –1560, translated
from the French by R. N. Currey.

THE LOVER, WHOSE MISTRESS FEAR-ED A MOUSE, DECLARETH THAT HE WOULD BECOME A CAT IF HE MIGHT HAVE HIS DESIRE.

IF I might alter kind,
   What, think you, I would be?
Not Fish, nor Foule, nor Fle, nor Frog
   Nor Squirrel on the Tree;
The Fish, the Hooke, the Foule
   The lymed Twig doth catch,
The Fle, the Finger, and the Frog
   The Bustard doth dispatch.

37

The Squirrel thinking nought,
    That feately cracks a nut;
The greedie Goshawke wanting prey,
    In dread of Death doth put;
But scorning all these kindes,
    I would become a Cat,
To combat with the creeping Mouse
    And scratch the screeking Rat.

I would be present, aye,
    And at my Ladie's call,
To gard her from the fearfull Mouse,
    In Parlour and in Hall;
In Kitchen, for his Lyfe,
    He should not shew his hed;
The Pease in Poke should lie untoucht
    When shee were gone to Bed.

The Mouse should stand in Feare,
    So should the squeaking Rat;
All this would I doe if I were
    Converted to a Cat.

        George Turberville, 1540?—1610.

FROST-EYEBROWS

IN the middle of the Chia-ching period [1522–
1566] there was a cat in the palace. She was
of faintly blue colour but her two eyebrows
were clearly jade-white and she was called
Frost-eyebrows. She surmised the Emperor's
intentions very well. Whomever His Majesty
summoned and wherever her Imperial master
went, she always led. She waited upon the
Emperor until he slept and then she lay still
like a stump. His Majesty was very fond of
her, and, when she died, ordered that she
should be buried in the north side of the Wan-

sui mountains in Peking. By her grave was erected a stone tablet inscribed: "Grave of a Dragon with two horns."

The *Great Encyclopedia of Ten Thousand Chapters*, 1725.

A WHITE GREAT NIMBLE CAT

I HAVE (and long shall have) a white great
   nimble cat,
A king upon a mouse, a strong foe to the
   rat,
Fine eares, long taile he hath, with Lions
   curbed clawe,
Which oft he lifteth up, and stayes his
   lifted pawe,
Deepe musing to himselfe, which after —
   mewing showes,
Till with lickt beard, his eye of fire espie
   his foes.

Sir Philip Sidney, 1554 – 1586.

CATS are of divers colours, but for the most part gryseld, like to congealed yse, which cometh from the condition of her meate: her head is like unto the head of a Lyon, except in her sharpe eares: her flesh is soft and smooth: her eyes glitter above measure especially when a man cometh to see a Cat on the sudden, and in the night, they can hardly be endured, for their flaming aspect. Wherefor Democritus describing the Persian smaradge saith that it is not transparent but filleth the eye with pleasant brightnesse, such as in the eyes of Panthers and Cats, for they cast forth beames in the shadow and darkness, but in the sunshine they have no such clearness and therefor Alexander Aphrodise giveth this reason, both for the sight of Cattes and Battes, that they have by nature a most sharp spirit of seeing.

Albertus compareth their eyesight to carbuncles in dark places, because in the night, they can see perfectly to kill Rattes and Myce: the roote of the herbe Valerian (commonly called Phu) is very like to the eye of a Cat, and wherefore it groweth if

42

cats come thereunto, they instantly dig it up, for the love thereof, as I myself have seene in mine owne Garden, and not once onely, but often, even then when I had caused it to be hedged or compassed round about with thornes, for it smelleth marveilous like to a cat.

The Egyptians hath observed in the eyes of a Cat, the encrease of the Moonlight, for with the Moone, they shine more fully at the ful, and more dimly in the change and wain, and the male Cat doth also vary his eyes with the sunne; for when the sunne ariseth, the apple of his eye is long; towards noone it is round, and at the evening it cannot be seene at all, but the whole eye sheweth alike.

The tongue of a Cat is very attractive, and forcible like a file, attenuating by licking the flesh of a man, for which cause, when she is come neere to the blood, so that her own spittle be mingled therewith, she falleth mad. Her teeth are like a saw, and if the long haires growing about her mouth (which some call Granons) be cut away, she looseth her courage. Her nailes sheathed like the nailes of a Lyon, striking with her fore-feete, both Dogs and other things, as a man doth with his hand.

The beast is wonderful nimble, setting upon her prey like the Lyon, by leaping : and therefore she hunteth both Rats, all kinds of Myce, and Birds, eating not only them, but also Fish, wherewith all she is best pleased. It is a neat and cleanely creature, oftentimes licking her own body to keepe it smoothe and faire, having naturally a flexible backe for this purpose, and washing her face with her fore-feete, but some observe that if she put her feete beyond the crowne of her head, that it is a presage of raine, and if the backe of a Cat be thinne, the beast is of no courage or value.

It is needlesse to spend any time about her loving nature to man, how she flattereth by rubbing her skinne against one's Legges, how she whurleth with her voyce, having as many tunes as turnes, for she hath one voyce to beg and complain, another to testify her delight and pleasure, another among her own kind by flattering, by hissing, by puffing, by spitting, insomuch as some have thought that they have a peculiar intelligible language among

themselves. Therefore how she beggeth, play-
eth, leapeth, looketh, catcheth, tosseth with
her foote, riseth up to strings held over her
head, sometimes creeping, sometimes lying
on the back, playing with one foot, sometimes
on the bely, snatching, now with the mouth,
and anon with foot, apprehending greedily
anything save the hand of a man with divers
such gestical actions, it is needelesse to stand
upon; insomuch as Cœlus was wont to say,
that being free from his Studies and more ur-
gent weighty affairs, he was not ashamed
to play and sport himself with his Cat, and
verily it might well be called an idle man's
pastime...

From *The Historie of Foure-Foot-
ed Beastes*, by Edward Topsell, 1607.

MONTAIGNE AND HIS CAT

THE learned and ingenious Montaigne
says like himself freely, "When my cat
and I entertain each other with mutual apish
tricks, as playing with a garter, who knows
but that I make my cat more sport than she
makes me? Shall I conclude her to be simple,

that has her time to begin or refuse to play as free as I myself have? Nay, who knows but that it is a defect of my not understanding her language (for doubtless cats talk and reason with one another) that we agree no better? And who knows but that she pities me for being no wiser than to play with her, and laughs and censures my folly for making sport for her, when we two play together?"

Thus freely speaks Montaigne concerning Cats.

From *The Compleat Angler* by Izaak Walton, 1593 – 1683.

THE POOR CAT I' THE ADAGE

C*ATUS* amant pisces, sed non vult tangere plantas.

F AIN would the cat fish eat, But she's loath to wet her feet.

Traditional.

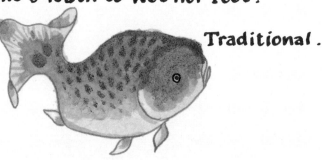

PERPLEXED CAT

LETTING "I dare not" wait upon "I would,"
Like the poor cat i' the adage.

William Shakespeare, 1564–1616.

COMPASSIONATE CAT

I THINK Crab my dog be the sourest-natured
dog that lives: my mother weeping, my
father wailing, my sister crying, our maid
howling, our cat wringing her hands, and all
our house in a great perplexity, yet did not
this cruel-hearted cur shed one tear.

William Shakespeare, 1564-1616.

THIRSTY CAT

THEY'LL take suggestions as a cat laps
milk.

William Shakespeare, 1564–1616.

MELANCHOLY CAT

'S BLOOD, I am as melancholy as a gib cat.

William Shakespeare, 1564–1616.

47

THESPIAN CAT

MACBETH, Act IV, Scene I, *A Cavern.*
Thunder. Enter the three Witches.
More thunder. Enter a Brinded Cat.

Brinded Cat. Miaow! Miaow! Miaow!
                [*Exit Brinded Cat.*
First Witch. Thrice the brinded cat
   hath mew'd.
Sec. Witch. Thrice and once the hedge-
   pig whin'd.
Third Witch. Harper cries: 'T is time,

48

'tis time.
First Witch. Round about the cauldron go;
In the poison'd entrails throw.
Toad, that under cold stone
Days and nights hast thirty-one
Swelter'd venom sleeping got,
Boil thou first i' the charmed pot.
All. Double, double toil and trouble
Fire burn and cauldron bubble....

William Shakespeare, 1564-1616.

VIGILANT CAT

I AM as vigilant as a cat to steal cream.

William Shakespeare, 1564-1616.

FIERCE CAT

THE cat, with eyne of burning coal,
Now couches fore the mouse's hole.

William Shakespeare, 1564-1616.

DISTINGUISHED CAT

BENVOLIO. Why, what is Tybalt?
Mercutio. More than a prince of cats,
I can tell you.
William Shakespeare, 1564-1616.

49

BETTER TO BE A CAT THAN A POP-SINGER

I HAD rather be a kitten and cry mew
Than one of these same metre ballad-
mongers.
              William Shakespeare, 1564-1616.

AILUROPHOBIA

S OME that are mad if they behold a cat
. . . a harmless, necessary cat.

           William Shakespeare, 1564-1616.

THE CAT OF Mr. W. H.

A VERY remarkable accident befel *Henry
Wriothesly*, earl of *Southampton*, the
friend and companion of the earl of *Essex*,
in his fatal insurrection: after he had been
confined here [the Tower of London] a
short time, he was surprized by a visit
from his favourite cat, which had found
its way to the *Tower*, and, as tradition
says, reached its master by descending
the chimney of his apartment. I have
seen at *Bulstrode*, the summer resid-

ence of the late duchess of *Portland*, an original portrait of this earl, in the place of his confinement in a black dress and cloak, with the faithful animal sitting by him.

Pennant's *Some Account of London*

Imagine the scene: this Douglas Fairbanks of a cat, swimming the moat; scaling the battlements; baffling the Beafeaters; wrestling with rats and running through ravens with his rapier claws; and, finally,

51

descending upon the unhappy prisoner—
like Leonora in *Fidelio*—in a shower of
soot and devotion. A Bravo Cat indeed!

It is impossible to suppose that Shakespeare, his imagination so keenly responsive
to tales of heroism and loyalty, did not compose a sonnet on this most adventurous and
well-wishing of *well-wishing adventurers*
setting forth. Over to you, Dr A.L. Rowse.

CARDINAL RICHELIEU

CARDINAL Richelieu, the Machiavell-
ian French minister of the 17th century,
was a fanatic cat-lover. He had dozens of
cats at court and his will included provision
for fourteen of his pets; alas, Swiss mer-
cenaries butchered them all for a gargant-
uan stew.

UPON A FRIEND'S PET CAT, BEING SICK

HOW fickle's Health! when sickness thus
So sharp, so sudden visits *Puss*!
A warning fair, and Instance good,
To show how frail are Flesh and Blood,

That Fate has Mortals at a Call,
Men, Women, Children — Cats and all.
Nor should we fear, despair, or sorrow,
If well to-day, and ill to-morrow,
Grief being but a Med'cine vain,
For griping Gut, or aking Brain,
And Patience the best Cure for Pain.
How brisk and well, last Week, was Puss!
How sleek, and plump, as one of us:
Yet now, alack! and well-a-day!
How dull, how rough, and fall'n away.
How feintly creeps about the House!
Regardless or of Play, or Mouse!
Nor stomack has, to drink, or eat,
Or sweetest Milk, or daintiest Meat;
A grievous this, and sore Disaster
To all the House, but most his Master,
Who sadly takes it thus to heart,
As in his Pains he bore a part.
And, what increases yet his Grief,
Is, nought can cure, or bring Relief,
No Doctor caring to prescribe,
Or Med'cine give, for Love, or Bribe,
No other Course, but to petition
Dame Nature, oft the best Physician,
The readiest too, and cheapest sure,

Since she ne'er asks a Fee for Cure
Nor ever takes a single Shilling,
As many basely do for killing.
So, for a while, snug let him lye,
As Fates decree, to live or dye,
While I, in dismal dogrel Verse,
His beauties and his Fame rehearse.
Poor *Bob*! how I have smiled to see
Thee sitting on thy Master's Knee?
While, pleased to stroke thy Tabby-coat,
Sweet Purrings warbling in thy Throat,
He would with rapturous Hug declare,
No Voice more sweet, or Maid more fair.
No prating Poll, or Monkey bold,
Was more caress'd by Woman old,
Nor flutt'ring Fop, with Am'rous Tongue
So much admir'd by Virgin Young.
Miss *Betty's* Bed-fellow, and Pet,
(Too young to have another yet),
At Dinner, he'd beside her sit,
Fed from her Mouth with sweetest Bit;
Nor Mrs. L——'s so charming *Philly*
Was more familiar, fond, or silly,
Nor Mrs. C——'s ugly Cur
Made more a foustre, or more stir.
Oft tir'd, and cloy'd, with being petted,
Or else by *Molly* beaten, fretted,

He'd out into the Garden run,
To sleep in th' Shade, or bask in th' Sun;
Sometimes about the Walks he'd ramble,
Or on the verdant Green would amble,
Or under the hedges sculking sit,
To catch the unwary *Wren*, or *Tit*,
Or *Sparrows* you, which Sun-beams hot
Had forc'd to quit their mansion Pot,
Then murther with relentless Claws.
Now, cruel Death, so fierce and grim,
With gaping jaws does threaten him,
While pining, he, with Sickness sore,
Oppress'd and griev'd, can hunt no more.

    Now joyful Mice skip, frisk, and play,
And safely revel, Night and Day.
The Garrets, Kitchens, Stairs, and Entry,
Unguarded by that dreadful Centry.

    The Pantry now is open set,
No fear for *Puss* therein to get,
With Chicken cold to run away,
Or sip the Cream set by for Tea;
Jenny now need not watch the Door,
Or for lost Meat repine no more,
Nor *Molly* many a scolding dread
For slamming him from off the Bed;
Poor harmless Animal! now lies
As who can say, he lives or dies.

Tho' I have heard a saying that
Some three times three Lives has a Cat;
Should Death then now the Conquest gain,
And feeble *Bob*, with struggle vain,
To his resistless Fate give way,
Yet come to Life, another Day,
How will Time scratch his old bald Pate,
To see himself so *Bobb'd*, so Bit,
To find that *Bob* has eight Lives more
To lose, e'er he can him secure.
Should he however, this Bout dye,
What Pen should write his Elegy?
No living Bard is fit, not One;
Since *Addison*, and *Parnel's* gone;
Or such another Pen, as that
Which wrote so fine on *Mountaign's* Cat.

John Winstanley, 1678—1751.

LORD CHESTERFIELD

LORD Chesterfield, of the famous letters to his illegitimate son, was devoted to cats, and in his will, dated 4th June, 1772, he bequeathed a sum for the maintenance of his favourite cat.

DR SAMUEL JOHNSON

NOR would it be just under this head, to omit the fondness which he showed for animals which he had taken under his protection. I never shall forget the indulgence with which he treated Hodge, his cat; for whom he himself used to go out and buy oysters, lest the servants having that trouble should take a dislike to the poor creature. I am, unluckily, one of those who have an antipathy to a cat, so that I am uneasy when in the room with one; and I own, I frequently suffered a good deal from the presence of the same Hodge. I recollect him one day scrambling up Dr. Johnson's breast, apparently with much satisfaction, while my friend, smiling and half-whistling, rubbed down his back, and pulled him by the tail; and when I observed he was a fine cat, say- "Why, yes, Sir, but I have had cats whom I liked better than this"; and then, as if perceiving Hodge to be out of counten-ance, adding, "but he is a very fine cat, a very fine cat indeed."

This reminds me of the ludicrous account which he gave Mr. Langton of the despicable

state of a young gentleman of good family .
"Sir, when I heard of him last, he was running about town, shooting cats." And then, in a sort of kindly reverie, he bethought himself of his own favourite cat, and said, "But Hodge shan't be shot: no, no, Hodge shall not be shot."

James Boswell, 1740-1795.

ON THE DEATH BY DROWNING OF HORACE WALPOLE'S CAT

Gray to Walpole

22nd February, 1747.

AS one ought to be particularly careful to avoid blunder in a compliment of condolence, it would be a sensible satisfaction to me (before I testify my sorrow, and the sincere part I take in your misfortune) to know for certain, who it is I lament. I knew Zara and Selima, (Selima, was it? or Fatima) or rather I knew them both together; for I cannot justly say which was which. Then as to your handsome

Cat, the name which you distinguished her
by, I am no less at a loss, as well knowing
one's handsome cat is always the cat one
likes best; or, if one be alive and the other
dead, it is usually the latter that is the
handsomest. Besides, if the point were
never so clear, I hope you do not think me so
ill bred or so imprudent as to forfeit all
my interest in the survivor....

1st March, 1747.

Heigh-ho! I feel that I have very little to
say, at least in prose. Somebody will be the
better for it; I do not mean you, but your
cat, feue Mademoiselle Selime, whom I am
about to immortalise for one week or fort-
night, as follows:

Ode
On the death of a favourite cat
Drowned in a tub of gold fishes

'Twas on a lofty vase's side
Where China's gayest art had dy'd
   The azure flowers that blow;
Demurest of the tabby kind,

The pensive Selima, reclin'd,
   Gaz'd on the lake below.

Her conscious tail her joy declar'd;
The fair round face, the snowy beard,
   The velvet of her paws,
Her coat, that with the tortoise vies,
Her ears of jet, and emerald eyes,
   She saw; and purr'd applause.

Still had she gaz'd; but 'midst the tide
Two angel forms were seen to glide,
   The Genii of the stream:
Their scaly armour's Tyrian hue
Thro' richest purple to the view
   Betray'd a golden gleam.

The hapless Nymph with wonder saw:
A whisker first, and then a claw,
   With many an ardent wish,
She stretch'd in vain to reach the prize.
What female heart can gold despise?
   What Cat's averse to fish?

Presumptuous Maid! with looks intent
Again she stretch'd, again she bent,
   Nor knew the gulf between.
(Malignant Fate sat by, and smil'd.)

The slipp'ry verge her feet beguil'd,
  She tumbled headlong in.

Eight times emerging from the flood
She mew'd to ev'ry wat'ry God,
  Some speedy aid to send.
No Dolphin came, no Nereid stirr'd:
Nor cruel *Tom*, nor *Susan* heard.
  A Fav'rite has no friend!

From hence, ye Beauties, undeceiv'd,
Know, one false step is ne'er retriev'd,
  And be with caution bold.
Not all that tempts your wand'ring eyes
And heedless hearts, is lawful prize;
  Nor all that glisters, gold.

MY CAT JEOFFRY

FOR I will consider my cat Jeoffry.
  For he is the servant of the living God,
    duly and daily serving him.
For at the first glance of the glory of God
    in the East he worships in his way.
For this is done by wreathing his body seven
    times round with elegant quickness.
For when he leaps up to catch the musk, which
    is the blessing of God upon his prayer.
For he rolls upon prank to work it in.
For having done duty and received blessing
    he begins to consider himself.
For this he performs in ten degrees.
For first he looks upon his fore-paws to see
    if they are clean.
For secondly he kicks up behind to clear away
    there.
For thirdly he works it upon stretch with
    the fore-paws extended.
For fourthly he sharpens his paws by wood.
For fifthly he washes himself.
For sixthly he rolls upon wash.
For seventhly he fleas himself, that he may
    not be interrupted upon the beat.
For eighthly he rubs himself against a post.

For ninthly he looks up for instructions.

For tenthly he goes in quest of food.

For having consider'd God and himself he will consider his neighbour.

For if he meets another cat he will kiss her in kindness.

For when he takes his prey he plays with it to give it a chance.

For one mouse in seven escapes by his dallying

For when his day's work is done his business more properly begins.

For he keeps the Lord's watch in the night against the adversary.

For he counteracts the powers of darkness by his electrical skin and glaring eyes.

For he counteracts the Devil, who is death, by brisking about the life.

For in his morning orisons he loves the sun and the sun loves him.

For he is of the tribe of Tiger.

For the Cherub Cat is a term of the Angel Tiger.

For he has the subtlety and hissing of a serpent, which in goodness he suppresses

For he will not do destruction, if he is well-

fed, neither will he spit without provoc-
ation.

For he purrs in thankfulness, when God tells
him he's a good Cat.

For he is an instrument for the children to
learn benevolence upon.

For every house is incompleat without him
& a blessing is lacking in the spirit.

For the Lord commanded Moses concerning the cats at the departure of the
Children of Israel from Egypt.

For every family had one cat at least in the
bag.

For the English cats are the best in Europe.

For he is the cleanest in the use of his fore-
paws of any quadrupeds.

For the dexterity of his defence is an instance of the love of God to him exceed-
ingly.

For he is the quickest to his mark of any
creature.

For he is tenacious of his point.

For he is a mixture of gravity and waggery.

For he knows that God is his Saviour.

For there is nothing sweeter than his peace
when at rest.

For there is nothing brisker than his life
    when in motion.
For he is of the Lord's poor and so indeed is
    he called by benevolence perpetually—
    Poor Jeoffry! poor Jeoffry! the rat has
    bit thy throat.
For I bless the name of the Lord Jesus that
    Jeoffry is better.
For the divine spirit comes about his body
    to sustain it in a compleat cat.
For his tongue is exceeding pure so that it
    has in purity what it wants in musick
For he is docile and can learn certain
    things.
For he can set up with gravity which is
    patience upon approbation.
For he can fetch and carry, which is pat-
    ience in employment.
For he can jump over a stick which is pat-
    ience upon proof positive.
For he can spraggle upon waggle at the
    word of command.
For he can jump from an eminence into his
    master's bosom.
For he can catch the cork and toss it again.
For he is hated by the hypocrite and miser.
For the former is afraid of detection.

For the latter refused the charge.
For he camels his back to bear the first mo-
	tion of business.
For he is good to think on, if a man would
	express himself neatly.
For he made a great figure in Egypt for his
	signal services.
For he killed the Icneumon-rat very perni-
	cious by land.
For his ears are so acute that they sting
	again.
For from this proceeds the passing quickness
	of his attention.
For by stroaking of him I have found out
	electricity.
For I perceived God's light about him both
	wax and fire.
For the Electrical fire is the spiritual sub-
	stance, which God sends from heaven
	to sustain the bodies both of man and
	beast.
For God has blessed him in the variety of his
	movements.
For, tho he cannot fly, he is an excellent
	clamberer.
For his motions upon the face of the earth
	are more than other quadrupeds.

For he can tread to all the measures upon
	the musick.
For he can swim for life.
For he can creep....

From *Rejoice in the Lamb: A Song from
Bedlam* by Christopher Smart, 1722–1771.

PARSON WOODFORDE CURES A CAT...

I HAD a poor little cat, that had one of her
ribs broke and that laid across her belly,
and we could not tell what it was, and she
was in great pain. I therefore with a small

pen knife this morning, opened one side of her and took it out, and performed the operation very well, and afterwards sewed it up and put Friars Balsam to it, and she was much better after, the incision was half an inch. It grieved me very much to see the poor creature in such pain before, and therefore made me undertake the above, which I hope will preserve the life of the poor creature.

Rev. James Woodforde, 26th October, 1768.

AND A CAT CURES PARSON WOODFORDE

THE Stiony on my right Eye-lid still swelled and inflamed very much. As it is commonly said that the Eye-lid being rubbed by the tail of a black Cat would do it much good if not entirely cure it, and having a black Cat, a little before dinner I made a trial of it, and very soon after dinner I found my Eye-lid much abated of the swelling and almost free from Pain. I cannot therefore but conclude it to be of the greatest service to a Stiony of the Eye-lid. Any other Cats Tail may have the

the above effect in all probability —but I did my Eye-lid with my own black Tom Cat's Tail.

Rev. James Woodforde, 11th March, 1791.

TEN LITTLE MICE

TEN little mice sat down to spin;
  Pussy passed by, and just looked in,
"What are you doing, my jolly ten?"
"We're making coats for gentlemen."
"Shall I come in and cut your threads?"
"No! No! Mistress Pussy—you'd bite off our
  heads."

Traditional.

LORD BYRON'S ESTABLISHMENT

Shelley to Thomas Love Peacock.

Ravenna, 10th August, 1821.

LORD Byron's establishment consists,
  beside servants, of ten horses, eight
enormous dogs, three monkeys, five cats, an
eagle, a crow, and a falcon; and all these,
except the horses, walk about the house,
which every now and then resounds with

their unarbitrated quarrels, as if they were the masters of it... After I have sealed my letters, I find that my enumeration of the animals in this Circean Palace was defective, and that in a material point. I have just met on the grand staircase five peacocks, two guinea hens, and an Egyptian crane. I wonder who all these animals were before they were changed into these shapes.

Percy Bysshe Shelley, 1792–1822.

TO A CAT

CAT! who hast passed thy grand climacteric,
How many mice and rats hast in thy days
 Destroy'd?—How many titbits stolen? Gaze
With those bright languid segments green and
 prick

Those velvet ears—but prithee do not stick
 Thy latent talons in me—and upraise
 Thy gentle mew—and tell me all thy frays
Of fish and mice, and rats and tender chick.
Nay, look not down, nor lick thy dainty wrists—
 For all the wheezy asthma,—and for all
Thy tail's tip is nick'd off—and though the
 fists
  Of many a maid have given thee many a
  maul,

Still is that fur as soft as when the lists
   In youth thou enter'dst on glass bottled
   wall.
                John Keats, 1795 – 1821.

OPERATIC CATS

THE beautiful and expressive voice of the cat has inspired fewer composers than, say, that of the nightingale; but Rossini's *Duetto Buffo di Due Gatti* is a tiny jewelled masterpiece. The work has only two characters, both coloratura soprano cats, and the entire opera, like *Tristan und Isolde*, is a love duet. The *libretto*, also by Rossini, consists of repetitions of the single word "Miau".

Stendhal reported Rossini's having been obliged, at Padua, to imitate a cat at 3 a.m. to get into a house he much wanted to enter. "A love adventure then," dryly comments Alfredo Bonaccorsi, the eminent musicologist.

THE POPE'S CAT

CHATEAUBRIAND'S most famous cat belonged previously to Pope Leo XII. In his memoirs, Chateaubriand writes:

The first moments of my sojourn in Rome were employed in official visits. His Holiness received me in private audience; public audiences are not customary and cost too dear. Leo XII, a Prince of tall stature and of an air at once serene and melancholy, is dressed in a plain white cassock; he maintains no pomp, and keeps to a poor room, almost unfurnished. He eats scarcely anything; he lives, with his cat, on a little polenta.

When the Pope died, Chateaubriand adopted his cat, and later took it with him to live in Paris. Writing there, in May, 1833, from his house in the garden of the Infirmerie de Marie-Thérèse, he relates:

I find myself at the same time in a Monastery, a farm, an orchard and a park. I have as a companion a fat red-grey cat with black cross stripes, born at the Vatican in the Raphael Gallery: Leo XII brought it up in the skirt of his robe, where I used to watch it with envy, when the Pontiff gave me my audience as Ambassador. On the death of the successor of St Peter, I inherited the cat without a master, as I have told you in writing of my Roman Embassy. They called it Micetto, surnamed the Pope's Cat. In this capacity it enjoys an extreme consideration among pious souls. I strive to make it forget exile, the Sistine Chapel and the sun of Michael Angelo's dome, on which it used to take its walks far removed from earth.

Popes Gregory XV and Pius IX were also ardently attached to their cats; and it is related that Pope Gregory the Great made *his* cat a cardinal.

PROSPER MÉRIMÉE ON CATS

I HAVE passed some pleasant and profitable hours in talking of cats with M. Prosper Mérimée, who loved them, and did not consider that he degraded himself as a man by acknowledging the intelligence of those animals. M. Mérimée would not admit, indeed, that they had any fault except an excessive sensitiveness. According to him, the cat proves its susceptibility by an extreme politeness, "In that," he said, "the animal resembles well-bred persons."

From *Les Chats* by Champfleury, 1821-89.

PRESIDENT LINCOLN RESCUES CATS

NOT long ago, too, General Horace Porter told of how Abraham Lincoln once found three motherless cats in a tent in General Grant's camp and forthwith took them under his coat and, in the midst of the crushing cares of that anxious time, saw to it that they were cared for.

Anecdote of the American Civil War.

OLD FOSS

WHEN staying at Cannes at Christmas, 1882, I was invited by Mr. Lear to go over to San Remo to spend a few days with him. Mr. Lear's villa was large, and the

second he had built; the first became unbearable to him from a large hotel having been
planted in front of it. So he put his new house
in a place by the sea, where, as he said, nothing could interrupt his light unless the
fishes built. The second house was exactly like the first. This, Mr. Lear explained
to me, was necessary or else Foss, his cat,
might not have approved of the new villa.
At breakfast the morning after I arrived,
this much-thought of, though semi-tailed,
cat jumped in at the window and ate a piece
of toast from my hand. This, I found, was
considered an event; when visitors stayed
at the Villa Tennyson, Foss generally hid
himself in the back regions; but his recognition of me was a sort of "guinea stamp"
which seemed to please Mr. Lear greatly,
and assured him of my fitness to receive the
constant acts of kindness he was showing
me.... He took from a place in his bureau a
number of carefully cut-out backs of old
envelopes, and on these he drew, to send
to my sister, then eight years old, the de-
lightful series of heraldic pictures of his
cat. After he had done seven he said it was
a great shame to caricature Foss, and

laid aside the pen.

Recounted by Henry Strachey.

Foss lived to the great age of seventeen years, during which he was his masters "daily companion." His master survived him by only a few months.

He has many friends, layman and clerical;
    Old Foss is the name of his cat;
His body is perfectly spherical,
    He weareth a runcible hat.

THE OWL AND THE PUSSY-CAT

THE owl and the Pussy-cat went to sea
    In a beautiful pea-green boat,
They took some honey, and plenty of money,
    Wrapped up in a five-pound note.
The owl looked up to the stars above,
    And sang to a small guitar,
"O lovely Pussy! O Pussy, my love,
    What a beautiful Pussy you are,
        You are,
        You are!
What a beautiful Pussy you are!"

Pussy said to the Owl, "You elegant fowl!
    How charmingly sweet you sing!
O let us be married! too long we have tarried:
    But what shall we do for a ring?"
They sailed away, for a year and a day,
    To the land where the Bong-tree grows
And there in a wood a Piggy-wig stood
    With a ring at the end of his nose,
        His nose,
        His nose,
With a ring at the end of his nose.

Dear Pig, are you willing to sell for one shilling
   Your ring?" Said the Piggy, "I will."
So they took it away, and were married next
   day
   By the Turkey who lives on the hill.
They dined on mince, and slices of quince,
   Which they ate with a runcible spoon;
And hand in hand, on the edge of the sand,
   They danced by the light of the moon,
      The moon,
      The moon,
They danced by the light of the moon.

Edward Lear, 1812—1888.

ATOSSA

CRUEL, but composed and bland,
Dumb, inscrutable and grand,
So Tiberius might have sat
Had Tiberius been a cat.

Matthew Arnold. 1822-1888.

THE CHESHIRE CAT

THE door led right into a large kitchen, which was full of smoke from one end to the other: the Duchess was sitting on a three-legged stool in the middle, nursing a baby: the cook was leaning over the fire, stirring a large cauldron which seemed to be full of soup.

"There's certainly too much pepper in that soup!" Alice said to herself, as well as she could for sneezing.

There was certainly too much of it in the *air*. Even the Duchess sneezed occasionally; and as for the baby, it was sneezing and howling alternately without a moment's pause. The only two creatures in the kitchen, that did *not* sneeze, were the cook, and a large cat, which was lying on the hearth and grinning from ear to ear.

"Please would you tell me," said Alice, a little timidly, for she was not quite sure whether it was good manners for her to speak first, "why your cat grins like that?"

"It's a Cheshire cat," said the Duchess, "and that's why. Pig!"

She said the last word with such sudden violence that Alice quite jumped; but she saw in another moment that it was addressed to the baby, and not to her, so she took courage, and went on again:—

"I didn't know that Cheshire cats always grinned; in fact, I didn't know that cats *could* grin."

"They all can," said the Duchess; "and most of 'em do."

"I don't know of any that do," Alice said very politely, feeling quite pleased to have got into a conversation.

"You don't know much," said the Duchess; "and that's a fact."

. . . She was a little startled by seeing the Cheshire Cat sitting on a bough of a tree a few yards off.

The Cat only grinned when it saw Alice. It looked good-natured, she thought: still it had *very* long claws and a great many teeth, so she felt it ought to be treated with respect.

"Cheshire Puss," she began, rather timidly, as she did not at all know whether it would like the name: however, it only grinned a little wider. "Come, it's pleased so far," thought Alice, and she went on. "Would you tell me, please, which way I ought to go from here?"

"That depends a good deal on where you want to get to," said the Cat.

"I don't much care where —" said Alice.

"Then it doesn't matter which way you go," said the Cat.

"— so long as I get *somewhere*," Alice added as an explanation.

"Oh, you're sure to do that," said the Cat, "if you only walk long enough."

Alice felt that this could not be denied, so she tried another question. "What sort of people live about here?"

"In *that* direction," the Cat said, waving its right paw round, "lives a Hatter: and in *that* direction," waving the other paw, "lives a March Hare. Visit either you like: they're both mad."

"But I don't want to go among mad people," Alice remarked.

"Oh, you ca'n't help that," said the Cat: "we're all mad here. I'm mad. You're mad."

"How do you know I'm mad?" said Alice.

"You must be," said the Cat, "or you wouldn't have come here."

Alice didn't think that proved it at all: however, she went on: "And how do you know that you're mad?"

"To begin with," said the Cat, "a dog's not mad. You grant that?"

"I suppose so," said Alice.

"Well, then," the Cat went on, "you see a dog growls when it's angry, and wags its tail when it's pleased. Now I growl when I'm pleased, and wag my tail when I'm angry. Therefore I'm mad."

"I call it purring, not growling," said Alice.

"Call it what you like," said the Cat. "Do you play croquet with the Queen to-day?"

"I should like it very much," said Alice, "but I haven't been invited yet."

"You'll see me there," said the Cat, and vanished.

Alice was not much surprised at this, she was getting so well used to queer things happening. While she was still looking at the place where it had been, it suddenly appeared again.

"By-the-bye, what became of the baby?" said the Cat. "I'd nearly forgotten to ask."

"It turned into a pig," Alice answered very quietly, just as if the Cat had come back in a natural way.

"I thought it would," said the Cat, and vanished again.

Alice waited a little, half expecting to see it again, but it did not appear, and after a minute or two she walked on in the direction in which the March Hare was said to live. "I've seen hatters before," she said to herself: "the March Hare will

be much the most interesting, and perhaps, as this is May, it won't be raving mad — at least not so mad as it was in March."
As she said this, she looked up, and there was the Cat again, sitting on a branch of a tree.

"Did you say 'pig', or 'fig?" said the Cat.

"I said 'pig,'" replied Alice; "and I wish you wouldn't keep appearing and vanishing so suddenly : you make one quite giddy!"

"All right," said the Cat; and this time it vanished quite slowly, beginning with the end of the tail, and ending with the grin, which remained some time after the rest of it had gone.

"Well! I've often seen a cat without a grin," thought Alice; "but a grin without a cat! It's the most curious thing I ever saw in all my life!"

. . . She was looking about for some way of escape, and wondering whether she could get away without being seen, when she noticed a curious appearance in the air: it puzzled her very much at first, but after watching it a minute or two she made it out to be a grin, and she said to herself, "It's the Cheshire Cat: now I shall have somebody to talk to."

"How are you getting on?" said the Cat, as soon as there was mouth enough for it to speak with.

Alice waited till the eyes appeared, and then nodded. "It's no use speaking to it," she thought, "till its ears have come, or at least one of them." In another minute the whole head appeared, and then Alice put down her flamingo, and began an account of the game, feeling very glad she had some one to listen to her. The Cat seemed to think that there was enough of it now in sight, and no more of it appeared.

"I don't think they play at all fairly," Alice began, in rather a complaining tone, "and they all quarrel so dreadfully one can't hear oneself speak — and they don't seem to have any rules in particular: at least, if there are, nobody attends to them — and you've no idea how confusing it is all the things being alive: for instance, there's the arch I've got to go through next walking about at the other end of the ground — and I should have croqueted the Queen's hedgehog just now, only it ran away when it saw mine coming!"

"How do you like the Queen?" said the Cat in a low voice.

"Not at all," said Alice: "she's so extremely —" Just then she noticed that the Queen was close behind her, listening: so she went on "—likely to win, that it's hardly worth while finishing the game."

The Queen smiled and passed on.

"Who *are* you talking to?" said the King, coming up to Alice, and looking at the Cat's head with great curiosity.

"It's a friend of mine — a Cheshire Cat," said Alice: "allow me to introduce it."

"I don't like the look of it at all," said the King: "however, it may kiss my hand, if it likes."

"I'd rather not," the Cat remarked.

"Don't be impertinent," said the King, "and don't look at me like that!" He got behind Alice as he spoke.

"A cat may look at a king," said Alice. "I've read that in some book, but I don't remember where."

"Well, it must be removed," said the King very decidedly; and he called to the Queen, who was passing at the moment, "My dear! I wish you would have this cat removed!"

The Queen had only one way of settling all difficulties, great or small. "Off with his head!" she said without even looking round.

"I'll fetch the executioner myself," said the King eagerly, and he hurried off.

. . . Alice went back to have a little more conversation with her friend.

When she got back to the Cheshire Cat, she was surprised to find a large crowd collected round it: there was a dispute going on between the executioner, the King, and the Queen, who were all talking at once, while all the rest were quite silent, and looking very uncomfortable.

The moment Alice appeared, she was

appealed to by all three to settle the question, and they repeated their arguments to her, though, as they all spoke at once, she found it very hard to make out exactly what they said.

The executioner's argument was, that you couldn't cut off a head unless there was a body to cut it off from: that he had never had to do such a thing before, and he wasn't going to begin at *his* time of life.

The King's argument was, that anything that had a head could be beheaded, and that you weren't to talk nonsense.

The Queen's argument was that, if something wasn't done about it in less than no time, she'd have everybody executed, all round. (It was this last remark that had made the whole party look so grave and anxious.)

Alice could think of nothing else to say but "It belongs to the Duchess: you'd better ask *her* about it."

"She's in prison," the Queen said to the executioner: "fetch her here." And the executioner went off like an arrow.

The Cat's head began fading away the moment he was gone, and, by the time he had come back with the Duchess, it had entirely disappeared: so the King and the executioner ran wildly up and down looking for it, while the rest of the party went back to the game.

Lewis Carroll, 1832—1898.

CATS

THE fervent lover and the sage austere
In their ripe season equally admire
The great soft cats, who, like their masters dear,
Are shivery folk and sit beside the fire.

Friends both of learning and of wantonness,
They hunt where silence and dread shadows are;
Erebus would have yoked them to his car
For funeral coursers had their pride been less.

They take, brooding, the noble attitudes
Of sphinxes stretched in deepest solitudes
That look to slumber in an endless dream:
Their loins are quick with kindlings magical,
And glints of gold, as in a sandy stream,
Vaguely bestar their eyeballs mystical.

Charles Baudelaire, 1821 – 67.*

A HOUSE WITHOUT A CAT

A HOUSE without a cat, and a well-fed,
well-petted, and properly revered cat,

*Translated from the French by D.S. MacColl.

may be a perfect house, perhaps, but how can it prove its title.

Mark Twain, 1835 — 1910.

TO A CAT

STATELY, kindly, lordly friend,
              Condescend
Here to sit by me, and turn
Glorious eyes that smile and burn,
Golden eyes, love's lustrous meed,
On the golden page I read.

All your wondrous wealth of hair,
              Dark and fair,
Silken-shaggy, soft and bright
As the clouds and beams of night,
Pays my reverent hand's caress
Back with friendlier gentleness.

Dogs may fawn on all and some
              As they come;
You, a friend of loftier mind,
Answer friends alone in kind.
Just your foot upon my hand
Softly bids it understand.

Algernon Swinburne, 1837 — 1909.

"THUS freely speaketh Montaigne concerning cats," says Izaak Walton, who plainly disapproved of such liberties. They are increasing; and I observe authors who speak concerning cats with a familiarity and a levity most distasteful. Mr. W. L. Alden, for instance, is reported to boast that he is "an honorary cat," much as if a man were to call himself an honorary member of the Roxburghe Club. In dealing with cats, this author permits himself great and disrespectful licence. Mr. Louis Robinson, also, in what he says about cats (in *Wild Traits in Tame Animals*), treats cats as if they were subject to the ordinary laws of evolution, as understood by popular science. These laws, at least in books and papers of popular science, seem to me a set of fairy tales. Mr. Mivart, devoting a whole volume to the cat, properly handles with respect an animal which was a kind of god long, long before the days of Moses. But my present contest is with Mr. Robinson.

What does this agreeable author really know, on sound documentary evidence, about the history of the domestic puss? He begins with its prehistoric period, which he fancifully constructs out of the habits of the tame animal. Now these habits vary in different cats. Thus a regretted friend of my own, a black cat with a great deal of retenue, never went near another cat's dish; while, if another cat approached his dish, he instantly retired. "More food," he seemed to say, "is not worth a wrangle." He withdrew from all forms of competition, like a dignified Royal cat in exile. On the other hand, many cats, and one of mine in particular, always desert their own platter (however tempting) for that of their neighbour. Which of these opposite traits is primitive? "In its natural state," says Mr. Robinson, "the cat is not in the habit of associating with greedy companions." But, if you give a cat the leg of a grouse, partridge, or other game bird, he does show signs of greed and ferocity, growling as he feeds. Therefore in his natural state, when he caught game birds, I conceive that the cat did associate with greedy companions and growled to keep them away, just as newspapers growl at foreign nations. How did cats acquire their taste for fish? Has anyone seen a wild cat angling?

...If we take the case of cats, they say little, but they think a great deal; they conduct trains of reasoning. I have read an anecdote told by Mrs. Frederick Harrison. An old lady cat felt that she was dying, before her kittens were weaned. She could hardly walk, but she disappeared one morning, carrying a kitten, and came back without it. Next day, quite exhausted, she did this with her two other kittens, and then died. She had carried each kitten to a separate cat, each of which was nourishing a family, and accepted the new fosterling. Can anything be wiser or more touching? This poor old cat had memory, reflection, reason. Though wordless, she was as much a thinking creature as any man who makes his last will and testament.

Other cats came, with kind enquiries, to visit a puss whose leg had been hurt in a rabbit trap. One of them, having paid her visit, went out, caught a rabbit, and brought it back to the sufferer. What sportsman could do more?

... Some cats are snobs, though not so many cats as dogs share this human infirmity. A lady had two cats; one was a drawing-room cat, the other a common kitchen cat. Both, simultaneously, had families. The drawing-room cat carried her kittens downstairs to be nursed by the common kitchen cat, but every day she visited the nursery several times. She was not quite heartless, but she had never read Jean-Jacques Rousseau, on the nursing of children, and she was very aristocratic....

Andrew Lang, 1844—1912.

M ONTAIGNE, Du Bellay, Chateaubriand, Balzac, Mérimée, Mallarmé, Gautier, Dumas, Zola, Catulle Mendès, Pierre Loti, Baudelaire, Sainte-Beuve, Taine, Victor Hugo, Anatole France, Verlaine . . . it would be hard to find a French author who was *not* devoted to cats. Colette has written whole novels with only cats for characters; and Huysmans, a keen Devil worshipper and a regular attender at Black Mass, whose "poisonous" but, of course, "fascinating" novel (I found it dull) *A Rebours* had such an unfortunate influence on Dorian Gray, found a healthier expression

for his mysticism in his love of cats, about
which he wrote at great length. What a pity
Dorian read the wrong book!

The Americans have Edgar Allan Poe,
Mark Twain and Don Marquis; the Italians
have Petrarch and Tasso, who wrote

sonnets to his cat when confined in a mad house (Tasso, not the cat); and the Germans have Goethe and Hoffman, whose talented cat Murr not merely appeared in many of Hoffman's tales — though not, sadly, in *The Tales of Hoffman* —, but wrote and published his own book of philosophic reflections, *Lebensansichten des Katers Murr*.

GILBERTIAN CATS

LORD Chancellors were cheap as sprats,
And Bishops in their shovel hats
Were plentiful as tabby cats —
    In point of fact, too many.

Sir W. S. Gilbert, 1836 —1911.

JEROME K JEROME ON CATS

WHAT jolly chaps they are! They are much superior to human beings as companions. They do not quarrel or argue with you. They never talk about them — selves, but listen to you while you talk about yourself, and keep up an appear —

ance of being interested in the conversation. They never make stupid remarks. They never observe to Miss Brown across a dinner-table, that they always understood she was very sweet on Mr. Jones (who has just married Miss Robinson). They never mistake your wife's cousin for her husband, and fancy that you are the father-in-law. And they never ask a young author with fourteen tragedies, sixteen comedies, seven farces, and a couple of burlesques in his desk, why he doesn't write a play.

They never say unkind things. They never tell us of our faults, "merely for our own good." They do not, at inconvenient moments, mildly remind us of our past follies and mistakes. They do not say, "Oh yes, a lot of use *you are*, if you are ever really wanted" — sarcastic like. They never inform us, like our *inamoratas* sometimes do, that we are not nearly so nice as we used to be. We are always the same to them.

They are always glad to see us. They are with us in all our humours. They are merry when we are glad, sober when we feel solemn, sad when we are sorrowful.

...And when we bury our face in our hands and wish we had never been born, they don't sit up very straight, and observe that we have brought it all upon ourselves. They don't even hope it will be a warning to us. But they come up softly; and shove their heads against us. If it is a cat, she stands on your shoulder, rumples your hair, and says, "Lor', I am sorry for you, old man," as plain as words can speak....

Jerome K. Jerome, 1859 –1927.

COWBOY CAT

WHEN I went into winter camp, I always took plenty of novels and tobacco, and usually a cat. A cat and a briar pipe were lots of company when a fellow spent months shut off from the world.

Jim Christian of J. A. Ranch, Panhandle.

FIN-DE-SIÈCLE CAT

IN a dim corner of my room for longer than
   my fancy thinks
A beautiful and silent Sphinx has watched
   me through the shifting gloom.

Inviolate and immobile she does not rise she
   does not stir
For silver moons are naught to her and
   naught to her the suns that reel.

Red follows grey across the air, the waves of
   moonlight ebb and flow
But with the Dawn she does not go and in
   the night-time she is there.

Dawn follows Dawn and Nights grow old
    and all the while this curious cat
Lies couching on the Chinese mat with eyes
    of satin rimmed with gold.

Upon the mat she lies and leers and on the
    tawny throat of her
Flutters the soft and silky fur or ripples
    to her pointed ears.

Come forth, my lovely seneschal! so
    somnolent, so statuesque!
Come forth you exquisite grotesque! half
    woman and half animal!

Come forth my lovely langorous Sphinx!
    and put your head upon my knee!
And let me stroke your throat and see your
    body spotted like the Lynx!

And let me touch those curving claws of
    yellow ivory and grasp
The tail that like a monstrous Asp coils
    round your heavy velvet paws!

A thousand weary centuries are thine
    while I have hardly seen
Some twenty summers cast their green
    for Autumn's gaudy liveries.

But you can read the Hieroglyphs on the
    great sand-stone obelisks,
And you have talked with Basilisks, and
    you have looked on Hippogriffs.

O tell me, were you standing by when
    Isis to Osiris knelt?
And did you watch the Egyptian melt her
    union for Antony

And drink the jewel-drunken wine and
    bend her head in mimic awe
To see the huge proconsul draw the
    salted tunny from the brine?

And did you mark the Cyprian kiss white
    Adon on his catafalque?
And did you follow Amenalk, the God of
    Heliopolis?

And did you talk with Thoth, and did you
    hear the moon-horned Io weep?
And know the painted kings who sleep
    beneath the wedge-shaped Pyramid?

Lift up your large black satin eyes which
    are like cushions where one sinks!
Fawn at my feet, fantastic Sphinx! and
    sing me all your memories!

Sing to me of the Jewish maid who wan-
    dered with the Holy Child,
And how you led them through the wild,
    and how they slept beneath your shade.

Sing to me of that odorous green eve when
    crouching by the marge
You heard from Adrian's gilded barge the
    laughter of Antinous

And lapped the stream and fed your drouth
    and watched with hot and hungry stare
The ivory body of that rare young slave
    with his pomegranate mouth!....

Who were your lovers? who were they who
 wrestled for you in the dust?
Which was the vessel of your Lust?
 What Leman had you, every day?

Did giant Lizards come and crouch before
 you on the reedy banks?
Did Gryphons with great metal flanks
 leap on you in your trampled couch?

Did monstrous hippopotami come sidling
 toward you in the mist?
Did gilt-scaled dragons writhe and twist
 with passion as you passed them by?

And from the brick-built Lycian tomb
 what horrible Chimera came
With fearful heads and fearful flame to
 breed new wonders from your womb?

Or had you shameful secret quests and
 did you harry to your home
Some Nereid coiled in amber foam with
 curious rock crystal breasts?

Or did you treading through the froth
    call to the brown Sidonian
For tidings of Leviathan, Leviathan or
    Behemoth?

Or did you when the sun was set climb
    up the cactus-covered slope
To meet your swarthy Ethiop whose body
    was of polished jet?

Or did you while the earthen skiffs drop-
    ped down the grey Nilotic flats
At twilight and the flickering bats flew
    round the temple's triple glyphs

Steal to the border of the bar and swim
    across the silent lake
And slink into the vault and make the
    Pyramid your lúpanar

Till from each black sarcophagus rose up
    the painted swathed dead?
Or did you lure unto your bed the ivory-
    horned Tragelaphos?

Or did you love the god of flies who
    plagued the Hebrews and was splashed
With wine unto the waist? or Pasht, who
    had green beryls for her eyes?...

Or did huge Apis from his car leap down
    and lay before your feet
Big blossoms of the honey-sweet and
    honey-coloured nenuphar?

How subtle-secret is your smile! Did
    you love none then? Nay, I know
Great Ammon was your bedfellow! He lay
    with you beside the Nile!

The river-horses in the slime trumpeted
    when they saw him come
Odorous with Syrian galbanum and
    smeared with spikenard and with thyme.

He came along the river bank like some
    tall galley argent-sailed,
He strode across the waters, mailed in
    beauty, and the waters sank.

He strode across the desert sand: he reached
    the valley where you lay:
He waited till the dawn of day: then touched
    your black breasts with his hand.

You kissed his mouth with mouths of flame:
    you made the hornèd god your own:
You stood behind him on his throne: you
    called him by his secret name....

White Ammon was your bedfellow! Your
    chamber was the steaming nile!
And with your curved archaic smile you
    watch his passion come and go....

Ten hundred shaven priests did bow to Am-
    mon's altar day and night,
Ten hundred lamps did wave their light
    through Ammon's carven house —and now

Foul snake and speckled adder with their
    young ones crawl from stone to stone
For ruined is the house and prone the great
    rose-marble monolith!...

The god is scattered here and there: deep
   hidden in the windy sand
I saw his giant granite hand still clenched
   in impotent despair. . . .

Go, seek his fragments on the moor and
   wash them in the evening dew,
And from their pieces make anew thy
   mutilated paramour!

Go, seek them where they lie alone and
   from their broken pieces make
Thy bruisèd bedfellow! And wake mad
   passions in the senseless stone! . . .

Away to Egypt! Have no fear. Only one
   God has ever died.
Only one God has let His side be wounded
   by a soldier's spear.

But these, thy lovers, are not dead. Still by
   the hundred-cubit gate
Dog-faced Anubis sits in state with lotus-
   lilies for thy head.

Still from his chair of porphyry gaunt
    Memnon strains his lidless eyes
Across the empty land, and cries each
    yellow morning unto thee....

Your lovers are not dead, I know. Thy will
    rise up and hear your voice
And clash their cymbals and rejoice and
    run to kiss your mouth! And so

Set wings upon your argosies! Set
    horses to your ebon car!
Back to your Nile! Or if you are grown
    sick of dead divinities

Follow some roving lion's spoor aross
    the copper-coloured plain,
Reach out and hale him by the mane and
    bid him be your paramour!

Couch by his side upon the grass and set
    your white teeth in his throat
And when you hear his dying note lash
    your long flanks of polished brass....

Get hence, you loathsome mystery! Hideous animal, get hence!
You wake in me each bestial sense, you
make me what I would not be.

You make my creed a barren sham, you
wake foul dreams of sensual life,
And Atis with his blood-stained knife
were better than the thing I am.

False Sphinx! False Sphinx! By reedy Styx
old Charon, leaning on his oar,
Waits for my coin. Go thou before, and leave
me to my crucifix,

Whose pallid burden, sick with pain,
watches the world with wearied eyes,
And weep for every soul that dies, and
weeps for every soul in vain.

From *The Sphinx* by Oscar Wilde,
1854 — 1900.

A CAD'S VIEW OF CATS

THREE proper Men out of five will always throw things at a cat.

Rudyard Kipling, 1865 —1936.

THE ACHIEVEMENT OF THE CAT

IN the political history of nations it is no uncommon experience to find States and peoples which but a short time since were in bitter conflict and animosity with each other, settled down comfortably on terms of mutual goodwill and even alliance. The natural history of the social developments of species affords a similar instance in

the coming-together of two once warring
elements, now represented by civilized man
and the domestic cat. The fiercely-waged
struggle which went on between humans
and felines in those far-off days when
sabre-toothed tiger and cave lion con-
tended with primeval man, has long ago
been decided in favour of the most fitly
equipped combatant — the Thing with a
Thumb — and the descendants of the dis-
possessed family are relegated to-day,
and for the most part, to the waste
lands of jungle and veld, where an exist-
ance of self-effacement is the only alter-
native to extermination. But the felis
catus, or whatever species was the ancestor of the modern domestic cat (a
vexed question at present), by a master-
stroke of adaptation avoided the ruin of
its race, and "captured" a place in the very
keystone of the conqueror's organization.
For not as a bond-servant or dependant
has this proudest of mammals entered
the human fraternity; not as a slave
like the beasts of burden, or a humble

campfollower like the dog. The cat is domestic only as far as suits its own ends; it
will not be kennelled or harnessed nor suff-
er any dictation as to its goings out or
comings in. Long contact with the human
race has developed in it the art of diplo-
macy, and no Roman Cardinal of mediæ
val days knew better how to ingratiate
himself with his surroundings than a cat
with a saucer of cream on its mental
horizon. But the social smoothness, the
purring innocence, the softness of the
velvet paw may be laid aside at a moment's notice, and the sinuous feline
may disappear, in deliberate aloofness,
to a world of roofs and chimney-stacks,
where the human element is distanced
and disregarded. Or the innate savage
spirit that helped its survival in the
bygone days of tooth and claw may
be summoned forth from beneath the
sleek exterior, and the torture-instinct
(common alone to human and feline)
may find free play in the death-throes
of some luckless bird or rodent. It
is, indeed, no small triumph to have

combined the untrammelled liberty of primeval savagery with the luxury which only a highly developed civilization can command; to be lapped in the soft stuffs that commerce has gathered from the far ends of the world; to bask in the warmth that labour and industry have dragged from the bowels of the earth; to banquet on the dainties that wealth has bespoken for its table, and withal to be a free son of nature, a mighty hunter, a spiller of life-blood. This is the victory of the cat. But besides the credit of success the cat has other qualities which compel recognition. The animal which the Egyptians worshipped as divine, which the Romans venerated as a symbol of liberty, which Europeans in the ignorant Middle Ages anathematized as an agent of demonology, has displayed to all ages two closely-blended characteristics — courage and self-respect. No matter how unfavourable the circumstances, both qualities

are always to the fore. Confront a child,
a puppy, and a kitten with sudden danger;
the child will turn instinctively for ass-
istance, the puppy will grovel in abject
submission to the impending visitation,
the kitten will brace its tiny body for a
frantic resistance. And disassociate
the luxury-loving cat from the atmos-
phere of social comfort in which it
usually contrives to move, and observe
it critically under the adverse condi-
tions of civilization — that civilization which can impel a man to the
degradation of clothing himself in
tawdry ribald garments and caper-
ing mountebank dances in the street
for the earning of the few coins that
keep him on the respectable, or non-
criminal, side of society. The cat of
the slums and alleys, starved, outcast,
harried, still keeps amid the prowlings
of its adversity the bold, free, panther-
tread with which it paced of yore the
temple courts of Thebes, still dis-
plays the self-reliant watchfulness

which man has never taught it to lay aside. And when its shifts and clever managings have not sufficed to stave off inexorable fate, when its enemies have proved too strong or too many for its defensive powers, it dies fighting to the last, quivering with the choking rage of mastered resistance, and voicing in its death-yell that agony of bitter remonstrance which human animals, too, have flung at the powers that may be; the last protest against a destiny that might have made them happy — and has not.

"Saki" (H. H. Munro), 1870 — 1916.

PROFESSORIAL CAT

DEAR old Carolus Fletcher of Magdalen, whose tongue could be as stern and biting as his heart was sympathetic.

Punctually at nine o'clock in the morning he would come into Hall, perch himself on "high table" with his cat and deliver to us those lectures which are known

to the world as his History of England.
Excellent as are the published volumes,
they do not contain his comments to his
cat which formed no small part of the
pleasure which his lectures gave us. While
his master stroked him, the cat, with ad-
miring and appreciative gaze, would listen
to such remarks as:

"Ah, Puss, Henry the Eighth, besides
whom I look upon Nero as an impassioned
philanthropist," or:

"Let no man deceive you, Puss, Elizabeth
founded a new Church."

On this latter occasion a man got up
and walked out. When the door closed behind him, Fletcher turned to his cat and
said, "From Keble, I presume, Puss, don't
you?"

From a description of Charles Fletcher,
M.A. (1857 – 1934), historian and
Fellow of All Souls and of Magdalen
College, Oxford, by the late Mr. H.E.
Counsell.

THE COLLEGE CAT

WITHIN those halls where student zeal
    Hangs every morn on learning's lips,
Intent to make its daily meal
    Of Tips,

While drones the conscientious Don
    Of Latin Prose, of Human Will,
Of Aristotle and of John
    Stuart Mill,

We mouth with stern didactic air:
    We prate of this, we rant of that:
While slumbers on his favourite chair
    The Cat!

For what is Mill, and what is Prose,
    Compared with warmth, and sleep, and food,
—All which collectively compose
    The Good?

Although thy unreceptive pose
    In presence of eternal Truth
No virtuous example shows
    To youth,

Sleep on, O Cat! serenely through
    My hurricanes of hoarded lore,
Nor seek with agitated mew
    The door:

Thy calm repose I would not mar,
    Nor chase thee forth in angry flight
Protesting loud (though some there are
    Who might),

Because to my reflective mind
    Thou dost from generations gone
Recall a wholly different kind
    Of Don,

Who took his glass, his social cup,
    And having quaffed it, mostly sat
Curled (metaphorically) up
    Like that!

Far from those scenes of daily strife
    And seldom necessary fuss
Wherein consists the most of life
    For us,

When Movements moved, they let them move:
    When Problems raged, they let them rage:
And quite ignored the Spirit of
    The Age.

Of such thou wert the proper mate,
    O peaceful-minded quadruped!
But liv'st with fellows up to date
    Instead —

With men who spend their vital span
    In petty stress and futile storm,
And for a recreation plan
    Reform:

Whom pupils ne'er in quiet leave,
    But throng their rooms in countless hordes:
Who sit from morn to dewy eve
    On Boards:

Who skim but erudition's cream,
    And con by night and cram by day
Such subjects as the likeliest seem
    To pay!

But thou, from cares like these exempt,
    Our follies dost serenely scan,
Professing thus thy just contempt
    For Man:

For well thou knowest, that wished-for goal
    Which still to win we vainly pine,
That calm tranquillity of soul
    Is thine!

        Alfred Denis Godley, 1856 —1925.

ON A CAT AGING

HE blinks upon the hearth-rug
And yawns in deep content,
Accepting all the comforts
That Providence has sent.

Louder he purrs, and louder,
In one glad hymn of praise,
For all the night's adventures,
For quiet, restful days.

Life will go on for ever,
With all that cat can wish;
Warmth, and the glad procession
Of fish, and milk and fish.

Only — the thought disturbs him —
He's noticed once or twice,
The times are somehow breeding
A nimbler race of mice.

Sir Alexander Gray, 1882 — 1961.

ALFRED DE MUSSET

ALFRED de Musset
Used to call his cat Pusset.
His accent was affected.
That was to be expected.

Maurice Hare, 1886 — 1967

MUSIC-LOVING CAT.

WILL someone explain to me why the
cat gets excited in a peculiar way,
if you whistle to yourself very softly on a

high note? I have tried it with English, Italian and German cats; there is no geographical difference among them: if a cat hears you whistling (particularly if you are whistling as high as you can the Barcarole from *The Tales of Hoffman*), she begins in a fascinated way to brush against you, jump up on to your knees, sniff with bewilderment at your lips and finally in some sort of amorous excitement she begins to gnaw passionately at your mouth or nose with an expression of voluptuous depravity; after that, of course, you stop, and then she begins to purr hoarsely and industriously like a tiny motor. I have thought about it many times, and to the present day I do not know from what ancient instinct a cat adores whistling; I can't think that in primeval ages there were occasions when tom-cats used to whistle very softly instead of howling in a metallic and coarse alto, as they do at the present day. Perhaps in those remote and savage ages there lived some feline deities who to their faithful ones whistled with magic charm, but this is merely hypothesis, and the musical enchantment referred to is one of the mysteries of the cat's soul.

Karel Capek, 1890 — 1938.

THE CATS OF ROME

I NEVER learned to know the mysterious substance of cats until I was in Rome, and that was because there I was not looking at one cat but at fifty, at a whole swarm of cats, at a real cats' basin round the Trajan column. There an old forum has been excavated, which forms a basin in the middle of the square; and on the bottom of that dry reservoir, among the broken columns and statues, lives the independent race of cats; they live upon fish offal which the good-natured Italians throw to them from above; they observe some sort of cult of the moon, and except for that they clearly do nothing. Well, there it was brought home to me that a cat is not simply a cat, but something mysterious and unfathomable; that a cat is a wild animal.

If you see two dozen cats on the move a sudden realization dawns upon you that a cat doesn't walk at all, she prowls. Among human beings a cat is merely a cat; among cats a cat is a prowling shadow in a jungle. Quite obviously a cat trusts human beings; but she doesn't trust a cat because she knows her better than we do. People say "Dog and Cat" as one form of social distrust; but I have often seen a very intimate friendship between a dog and a cat, while I have never observed any intimacy between two cats, if, of course, we are not speaking of feline amours. The cats in Trajan's forum ignore one another most conspicuously: if they sit on the same column they sit back to back, nervously flicking their tails to make it understood that they find it hard to tolerate the presence of the slattern behind. When a cat looks at a cat she hisses; if they meet they don't turn back after each other; they never have a common purpose; they never have

127

anything to say to each other. At best
they tolerate each other in scornful and
negative silence.

Karel Capek, 1890 —1938.

ST JEROME AND HIS LION

ST Jerome in his study kept a great big
cat,
It's always in his pictures, with its feet
upon the mat.
Did he give it milk to drink, in a little
dish?
When it came to Fridays, did he give it fish?

If I lost my little cat, I'd be sad without it;
I should ask St. Jeremy what to do about it;
I should ask St Jeremy, just because of that,
For he's the only saint I know who kept
    a pussy cat.

Anonymous.

OTHER SAINTS AND CATS

ANOTHER saint who kept a pussy cat
was St Philip Neri (1515 – 1595). Cardinal Alfonso Capecelatro remarks:

He left his cat in his cell at S. Girolamo,
that she might serve as an occasion of continual mortification to himself and to others,
and she served his purpose well. He would
bid now one and now another of his disciples,
often men of great learning or high rank, take
the key to go to S. Girolamo to see how the cat
was, and take her some food, and bring him
back word whether she was comfortable and
contented. On their return he would ask, even
in the presence of Cardinals and other great
personages: "Well, so you have been to see
my dear cat? What nice dinner did you take
her? Is she well? Did she look happy and

comfortable? Had she a good appetite?"
Archbishop Laud (1573 – 1645), an *Anglican*
saint and martyr, was also "very sound on cats."
John Aubrey reports: "W. Laud, A. B. Cant. was
a great lover of Catts, He was presented with
some Cyprus-catts, i.e. our Tabby-catts, which
were sold, at first for 5 pounds a piece: this
was about 1637." —The fashion thus started
resulted in a change which Aubrey strongly
resented. "I doe well remember," he says cross-
ly, "that the common English Catt, was white
with some blewish piednesse: sc. a gallipot blew.
The race or breed of them is now almost lost."

FELIS SEMPER FELIX

FELIX kept on walking, walking....
From Pat Sullivan's *Felix the Cat*, 1921.

130

the song of mehitabel

i have had my ups and downs
but wotthehell wotthehell
yesterday sceptres and crowns
fried oysters and velvet gowns
and today i herd with the bums
but wotthehell wotthehell
i wake the world from sleep
as i caper and sing and leap
when i sing my wild free tune
wotthehell wotthehell
under the blear eyed moon
i am pelted with cast off shoon
but wotthehell wotthehell

do you think that i would change
my present freedom to range
for a castle or moated grange
wotthehell wotthehell
cage me and i d go frantic
my life is so romantic
capricious and corybantic
and i m toujours gai toujours gai

i know that i am bound
for a journey down the sound
in the midst of a refuse mound
but wotthehell wotthehell
oh i should worry and fret
death and i will coquette
there s a dance in the old dame yet
toujours gai toujours gai

i was once an innocent kit
wotthehell wotthehell
with a ribbon my neck to fit
and bells tied onto it
o wotthehell wotthehell
but a maltese cat came by
with a come hither look in his eye
and a song that soared to the sky
and wotthehell wotthehell
and i followed adown the street
the pad of his rhythmical feet
o permit me again to repeat
wotthehell wotthehell

my youth i shall never forget
but there s nothing i really regret
wotthehell wotthehell

there s a dance in the old dame yet
toujours gai toujours gai
the things that i had not ought to
i do because i ve gotta
wotthehell wotthehell
and i end with my favourite motto
toujours gai toujours gai

Don Marquis, 1878 –1937.

mehitabel s extensive past

mehitabel the cat claims that
she has a human soul
also and has transmigrated
from body to body and it
may be so boss you
remember i told you she accused
herself of being cleopatra once i
asked her about antony
anthony who she asked me
are you thinking of that
song about rowley and gammon and
spinach heigho for anthony rowley

no i said mark antony the
great roman the friend of
caesar surely cleopatra you

133

remember j caesar

listen archy she said i
have been so many different
people in my time and met
so many prominent gentlemen i
wont lie to you or stall i
do get my dates mixed sometimes
think of how much i have had a
chance to forget and i have
always made a point of not
carrying grudges over
from one life to the next archy

i have been
used something fierce in my time but
i am no bum sport archy
i am a free spirit archy i
look on myself as being
quite a romantic character oh the
queens i have been and the
swell feeds i have ate
a cockroach which you are
and a poet which you used to be
archy couldn t understand
my feelings at having come

down to this i have
had bids to elegant feeds where poets
and cockroaches would
neither the one be mentioned without a
laugh archy i have had
adventures but i
have never been an adventuress
one life up and the next life
down archy but always a lady
through it all and a
good mixer too always the
life of the party archy but never
anything vulgar always free footed
archy never tied down to
a job or housework yes looking
back on it all i can say is
i had some romantic
lives and some elegant times i
have seen better days archy but
what is the use of kicking kid its
all in the game like a gentleman
friend of mine used to say
toujours gai kid toujours gai he
was an elegant cat he used
to be a poet himself and he made up
some elegant poetry about me and him

lets hear it i said and
mehitabel recited

persian pussy from over the sea
demure and lazy and smug and fat
none of your ribbons and bells for me
ours is the zest of the alley cat
over the roofs from flat to flat
we prance with capers corybantic
what though a boot should break a slat
mehitabel us for the life romantic

we would rather be rowdy and gaunt and free
and dine on a diet of roach and rat

roach i said what do you
mean roach interrupting mehitabel
yes roach she said that s the
way my boy friend made it up
i climbed in amongst the typewriter
keys for she had an excited
look in her eyes go on mehitabel i
said feeling safer and she
resumed her elocution

we would rather be rowdy and gaunt and free
and dine on a diet of roach and rat
than slaves to a tame society
ours is the zest of the alley cat

fish heads freedom a frozen sprat
dug from the gutter with digits frantic
is better than bores and a fireside mat
mehitabel us for the life romantic

when the pendant moon in the leafless tree
clings and sways like a golden bat
i sing its light and my love for thee
ours is the zest of the alley cat
missiles around us fall rat a tat tat
but our shadows leap in a ribald antic
as over the fences the world cries scat
mehitabel us for the life romantic

persian princess i don t care that
for your pedigree traced by scribes pedantic
ours is the zest of the alley cat
mehitabel us for the life romantic

aint that high brow stuff
archy i always remembered it
but he was an elegant gent
even if he was a high brow and a
regular bohemian archy him and
me went aboard a canal boat
one day and he got his head into
a pitcher of cream and couldn't get
it out and fell overboard

he come up once before he
drowned toujours gai kid he
gurgled and then sank for ever that
was always his words archy toujours
gai kid toujours gai i
have known some swell gents
in my time dearie

Don Marquis, 1878 – 1937.

THE PET DEPARTMENT

Q. Our cat, who is thirty-five, spends
all of her time in bed. She follows every
move I make, and this is beginning to get

me. She never seems sleepy nor particularly happy. Is there anything I could give her?

Miss L. Mc.

A. There are no medicines which can safely be given to induce felicity in a cat, but you might try lettuce, which is a soporific, for the wakefulness. I would have to see the cat watching you to tell whether anything could be done to divert her attention.

Q. We have cats the way most people

have mice.

Mrs. C. L. Footloose.

A. I see you have. I can't tell from your communication, however, whether you wish advice or are just boasting.

James Thurber, 1894 —1961.

THE RUM TUM TUGGER

THE Rum Tum Tugger is a Curious Cat:
  If you offer him pheasant he would rather
    have grouse.
If you put him in a house he would much pre-
    fer a flat,
If you put him in a flat then he'd rather have
    a house.
If you set him on a mouse then he only wants
    a rat,
If you set him on a rat then he'd rather chase
    a mouse.
Yes the Rum Tum Tugger is a Curious Cat—
  And there isn't any call for me to shout it:
    For he will do
    As he do do
      And there's no doing anything about it!

The Rum Tum Tugger is a terrible bore:
When you let him in, then he wants to be out;
He's always on the wrong side of every door,
And as soon as he's at home, then he'd like
        to get about.
He likes to lie in the bureau drawer,
But he makes such a fuss if he can't get out.
Yes the Rum Tum Tugger is a Curious Cat—
    And it isn't any use for you to doubt it:
        For he will do
        As he do do
            And there's no doing anything about it!

The Rum Tum Tugger is a curious beast:
His disobliging ways are a matter of habit.
If you offer him fish then he always wants a
        feast;
When there isn't any fish then he won't eat
        rabbit.
If you offer him cream then he sniffs and
        sneers,
For he only likes what he finds for himself;
So you'll catch him in it right up to the ears,
If you put it away on the larder shelf.

The Rum Tum Tugger is artful and knowing,
The Rum Tum Tugger doesn't care for a
    cuddle;
But he'll leap on your lap in the middle of
    your sewing,
For there's nothing he enjoys like a horr-
    ible muddle.
Yes the Rum Tum Tugger is a Curious Cat—
    And there isn't any need for me to spout it:
        For he will do
        As he do do
            And there's no doing anything about it!

            T. S. Eliot, 1888 —1965.

BUSTOPHER JONES: THE CAT ABOUT TOWN

BUSTOPHER Jones is *not* skin and bones—
In fact, he's remarkably fat.
He doesn't haunt pubs—he has eight or nine
    clubs,
For he's the St. James's Street Cat!
He's the Cat we all greet as he walks down
    the street
In his coat of fastidious black:
No commonplace mousers have such well-
    cut trousers
Or such an impeccable back.
In the whole of St James's the smartest
    of names is
The name of this Brummell of Cats;
And we're all of us proud to be nodded or
    bowed to
By Bustopher Jones in white spats!

His visits are occasional to the *Senior*
    Educational
And it's against the rules
For any Cat to belong to both that

And the *Joint Superior Schools*.
For a similar reason, when game is in
    season
He is found, not at *Fox's*, but *Blimp's*;
But he's frequently seen at the gay *Stage
    and Screen*
Which is famous for winkles and shrimps.
In the season of venison he gives his
    ben'son
To the *Pothunter's* succulent bones;
And just before noon's not a moment too
    soon
To drop in for a drink at the *Drones*.
When he's seen in a hurry there's prob-
    ably curry
At the *Siamese* — or at the *Glutton*;
If he looks full of gloom then he's lunched
    at the *Tomb*
On cabbage, rice pudding and mutton.

So, much in this way, passes Bustopher's
    day —
At one club or another he's found.
It can be no surprise that under our eyes
He has grown unmistakably round.

He's a twenty-five pounder, or I am a bounder,
And he's putting on weight every day:
But he's so well preserved because he's
    observed
All his life a routine, so he'd say.
Or, to put it in rhyme: "I shall last out my
    time"
Is the word for this stoutest of Cats.
It must and it shall be Spring in Pall Mall
While Bustopher Jones wears white spats!

T. S. Eliot, 1888 — 1965.

WAR CAT

I AM sorry, my little cat, I am sorry—
If I had it, you should have it;
But there is a war on.

No, there are no table-scraps;
there was only an omelette
made from dehydrated eggs,
and baked apples to follow,
and we finished it all.
The butcher has no lights,
the fishmonger has no cod's heads—
there is nothing for you
but cat-biscuit
and those remnants of yesterday's ham;
you must do your best with it.

Round and pathetic eyes,
baby mouth opened in a reproachful cry,
how can I explain to you?
I know, I know:
"Mistress, it is not nice;
the ham is very salt
and the cat-biscuit very dull,
I sniffed at it, and the smell was not en-
    ticing.

Do you not love me any more?
Mistress, I do my best for the war-effort;
I killed four mice last week,
yesterday I caught a young stoat,
you stroked and praised me,
you called me a clever cat,
What have I done to offend you?
I am industrious, I earn my keep;
I am not like the parrot, who sits there
using bad language and devouring
parrot-seed at eight-and-sixpence a pound
without working for it.
If you will not pay me my wages
there is no justice;
If you have ceased to love me
there is no charity.

"See, now I rub myself against your legs
to express my devotion,
which is not altered by any unkindness.
My little heart is contracted
because your goodwill is withdrawn from me;
my ribs are rubbing together
for lack of food,
but indeed I cannot eat this —
my soul revolts at the sight of it.

I have tried, believe me,
but it was like ashes in my mouth.
If your favour is departed
and your bowels of compassion are shut up,
then all that is left me
is to sit in a draught on the stone floor
    and look miserable
till I die of starvation
and a broken heart."

Cat with the innocent face,
What can I say?
Everything is very hard on everybody.
If you were a little Greek cat,
or a little Polish cat,
there would be nothing for you at all,
not even cat-food:
indeed, you would be lucky
if you were not eaten yourself.
Think if you were a little Russian cat
prowling among the cinders of a deserted city!
Consider that pains and labour
and the valour of merchant-seamen and
    fishermen
have gone into the making of this biscuit
which smells so unappetising.
Alas! there is no language

in which I can say these things.

Well, well!
if you will not be comforted
we will put the contents of your saucer
into the chicken-bowl — there!
all gone! nasty old cat-food —
The hens, I dare say,
will be grateful for it.

Wait only a little
and I will go to the butcher
and see if by any chance
he can produce some fragments of the
      insides of something.

Only stop crying
and staring in that unbearable manner—
as soon as I have put on my hat
we will try to do something about it.

My hat is on,
I have put on my shoes,
I have taken my shopping basket —
What are you doing on the table?

The chicken-bowl is licked clean;
there is nothing left in it at all.

Cat,
hell-cat, Hitler-cat, human,
all-too-human cat,
cat corrupt, infected,
instinct with original sin,
cat of a fallen and perverse creation,
hypocrite with the innocent and limpid eyes—
is nothing desirable
till somebody else desires it?

Is anything and everything attractive
so long as it is got by stealing?
Furtive and squalid cat,
green glance, squinted over a cringing
    shoulder,
streaking hurriedly out of the back door
in expectation of judgment,
your manners and morals are perfectly
        abhorrent to me,
you dirty little thief and liar.

Nevertheless,
although you have made a fool of me,
yet, bearing in mind your pretty wheedling
    ways
(not to mention the four mice and the

immature stoat),
and having put on my hat to go to the
      butcher's,
I may as well go.

                Dorothy L. Sayers, 1893–1957.

CONFESSION

I'VE been named Poosie, and
   I am spoiled
Thoroughly, thoroughly spoiled, and I like it.
And don't let anyone tell you different.
I lie upon the softest cushions,
Under the downiest covers
And I love every moment.
I get the cream off the top of the milk every day
And special double thick, heavy on Sundays,
And I lap it up.
My owner is besotted.
She hugs and kisses me
And carries me around with her all day,
And talks to me
And I enjoy it.
I'm spoiled rotten, and, friends,
That's the life.

Whatever I want, I cry for,
Crab, lobster, caviare, fish roes, sardines,
    filet, white meat of chicken,
You name it,
She's got it,
I get it.
I don't want to work, or hunt.
If ten snow-white mice were to saunter
    past my nose,
I wouldn't lift a paw.
I'm greedy, graceless, shameless, lazy,
And luxury loving.
Everything that comes my way I take,
And yell for more.
I'm spoiled useless.
I admit it.
And I love it.

Paul Gallico, 1897–1976

APPLICATION

AHEM!
I am available.
I have no home,
No friends,

And no immediate prospects.

Not to give you a hardluck story,
But things have not been going so well
    with me lately.
I had a nice family
But the old lady died
And the man hated cats
So I went.

You can see I know how to look after myself,
Though I don't know for how much longer
In a filthy street
And no decent place to clean up.
I've been used to good things.

Housebroken? Of course,
Completely.
I am rather loyal.
I would be your cat —
Show it, I mean
When people come to visit,
By making a fuss over you,
And responding when you called me.

I'm not too finicky about food,
Food! Oh dear!
My stomach is empty

And my heart desolate.

I'm not meant to be a street cat,
Or make myself a furtive shadow
In an alley.
I'm lonely, lonely, lonely,
And frightened!
Please may I come in?

Paul Gallico, 1897–1976

MORE ROMAN CATS

THE great faunal glory of Rome is
The Cats. The souls of the more
evil Roman Emperors are supposed to have
returned in the form of cats to haunt the
scenes of their sinful pleasures. Certainly, one ca'n't but notice a wicked
gleam in their eyes; and the smirk of a
voluptuary still lingers about their whis-
kers.

Ancient Roman Cats lord it among the
ruins of the Forum, where they are fed
at midday by a Franciscan monk under the
Arch of Titus; Medieval Cats slink around
the Piazza del Paradiso; Renaissance

154

Cats swagger behind the Pantheon; and modern layabout cats have their pads in an over-spill cats-town in the *Piazza Vittoria*. They live on Social Security and Government handouts.

Cats are Honorary Roman Citizens; and no-one may harm them.

Walter Payne, M.A., 1926 —.

COOL CAT

"LIKE, pussy cat, pussy cat, where is you was?"

"Like, I was at Beaulieu to get all that jazz."

"Like, pussy cat, pussy cat, what happened there?"

"Like, if you don't know, man, you must be a square!"

Michael Myer, 1960.

APPENDIX

SQUALID THINGS

THE back of a piece of embroidery.
The inside of a cat's ear.
A swarm of mice, who still have no fur,
when they come wriggling out of their
nest.
The seams of a fur robe that has not
yet been lined.
Darkness in a place that does not give
the impression of being very clean.
A rather unattractive woman who looks
after a large brood of children.

From the *Pillow Book* of Sei Shōnagon,
Court Lady in tenth-century Japan.

157

A CAT WHO LIKES TO BE KING

STORE boss Mr Miles Baddeley puts out one of his two pet cats at night.

Monday, the black tom, is shown the back door. But Khan sleeps at the bottom of his master's bed.

Mr Baddeley, 38, is not inclined to argue. For Khan is a 60 lb mountain lion with not the best of tempers.

"I'm afraid he is very much the boss," said Mr Baddeley at his home in Heaton Moor Rd, Stockport. "If he does not get his own way he tends to become grumpy and sullen."

But so far, after eight months in his home, Khan has done no more than eat all the house plants.

Mr Baddeley said: "He is very little trouble apart from the £5 a week he costs me in rabbits and pigeons for his food."

Khan, two years old, is taken for walks at the end of a rope but his owner says neighbours have nothing to fear if he did get out.

Mr Baddely acquired Khan when his previous owner left the country and had to leave him behind.

Now he sees no reason why they should part company.

Tony Brooks, *Daily Express*, Monday, October, 1974.

CAT VERSUS BIRD

THE problem of the cat versus the bird is as old as time. If we attempt to resolve it by legislation, who knows but what we may be called upon to take sides as well in the age-old problem of dog versus cat, bird versus bird, or even bird versus worm. In my opinion the State of Illinois and its local governing bodies already have enough to do without trying to control feline delinquency.

Adlai Stevenson.

ACKNOWLEDGEMENTS

The author and publishers wish to thank the following who have kindly given permission for the use of copyright material.

Faber & Faber Ltd. for 'The Rum Tum Tugger' and 'Bustopher Jones: the Cat about Town' from *Old Possum's Book of Practical Cats* by T. S. Eliot;

Hamish Hamilton Ltd. and Rosemary A. Thurber for material from 'The Pet Department' from *The Owl in the Attic* by James Thurber, Harper & Row and Hamish Hamilton, 1963. Copyright © 1931, 1959 by James Thurber and 1961, the Estate of James Thurber;

David Higham Associates on behalf of the author's Estate for 'War Cat' by Dorothy L. Sayers;

Oxford University Press for 'Squalid Things' from *The Pillow Book of Sei Shonagon*, translated and edited by Ivan Morris (OUP 1967). Copyright © Ivan Morris 1967;

Souvenir Press Ltd. for 'Application' and 'Confession' by Paul Gallico.

Every effort has been made to trace all the copyright holders but if any have been inadvertently overlooked the publishers will be pleased to make the necessary arrangement at the first opportunity.